The Mayor
of
Kalymnos

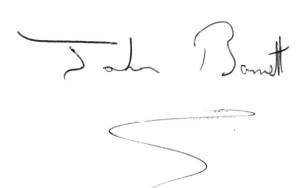

The Mayor
of
Kalymnos

By John Barrett

www.themayorofkalymnos.com

The Mayor of Kalymnos
By John Barrett

www.themayorofkalymnos.com

First Imprint: JC Studio Press 2022
Cover Photography: John Barrett
Design: Jane Cornwell ~ www.janecornwell.co.uk
Typeset in Adobe Lato.

ISBN: 978-1-7398281-8-9
Also available in paperback and ebook format.

Contents

Telendos.

For Maria, Hope, Lauren and Jackson

With special thanks to
Moyra Forrest and Graham Stein

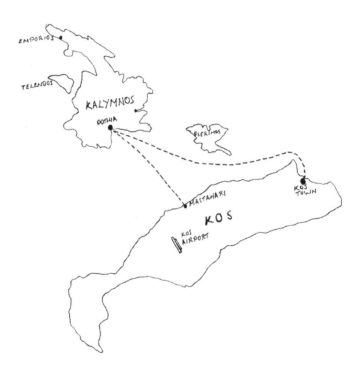

Pothia, Kalymnos, Greece.

Chapter 1
Kalymnos

A burning sensation in the middle of his back startled John. He sat bolt upright to see what was going on and where this intense heat was coming from. Was something on fire? - was he on fire? In the split second before his eyes opened, he realised that there was no smell of smoke and he was breathing fresh air, so he did not feel any immediate danger. A smile spread across his face as he turned to face the heat source.

As his blurred vision came into focus, he caught his first glimpse of the bright light and source of the burning heat. Through the window there was an intense light, the sun was rising in the east, creeping over the craggy mountain ridges and the blue and white-painted hilltop monasteries, on the Greek island of Kalymnos.

The window shutters had been left open from the night before, to allow what little breeze there was to cool his bedroom by a few degrees. The morning rays, which felt like a heat lamp at full power on his back, wakened him long before his alarm clock did. After the coldest winter on record, his life in Scotland had not prepared him for the heat of a Greek summer.

His eyes closed again, and he could now hear the island wakening up. The call of a cockerel was the first sound of the day. He smiled to himself, as this was what he had hoped for, a complete contrast to his old life, commuting every week between Edinburgh and London. Constantly on the move, busy with endless meetings and a relentless tide of email, always in the public eye and never finding time to wind down. Reluctantly he had recently invested in an iPod to drown out the constant background rumble of traffic while commuting. Although the technology was up to the minute; the music on it was not. What he wanted to hear now was the sound of silence. This was the perfect morning sound for what he felt was going to be the start of a tranquil few months, relaxing after many hectic years in Parliament and the manic activity of the recent General Election and its aftermath, which saw him become part of the negotiating process to form the new Government of the country – although he would now take no part in it. He felt that his work there was done.

Lying in bed, the sound of the lone cockerel was soon joined by a barking dog and a few more cockerels; the small town of Pothia was coming to life. John's senses were picking out the distant background noises, when, what sounded like a car crash, with the buckling of metal and loud excitable male voices shouting out in total panic tore into the room from what felt like only metres away. Grabbing his shorts and hopping on one leg, he tried to run and put them on at the same time. He snatched his mobile phone on the way to the balcony, ready to call the emergency services. He rushed outside, expecting to see carnage, only to see a startled look on the faces of the bin men, emptying the communal bin and wondering why the strange-looking white-skinned foreigner had both legs in the one leg of his pants. He looked at his phone, the clock said 5 am. They had started long before the day became too hot for physical work.

He smiled at them, they shrugged their hairy shoulders and carried on with their work, he went back to bed, but not to sleep.

The sounds from the cockerels and dogs had been joined by the first voices and vehicles of the day. The enjoyable country sounds were now being overtaken by an increasingly loud urban racket. The constant buzzing noise of the motorbikes with no silencers was drowned out only by the ear-shattering din of ready-mix concrete lorries struggling to climb the steep incline outside, while the blacksmith's workshop across the road, cutting metal with grinders and sounding like they were dropping steel from a great height every five minutes, now provided the constant rhythm upon which the cacophony from hell then developed. Time to get up, he thought.

As with many men in their 50s his morning routine now took slightly longer than before. There was more to deal with, with hair now appearing everywhere, apart from where it was wanted, on the top of his head. His eyebrows, ears and nose hair had all taken on a new lease of life, and although he could not see too much difference in the thickness of hair on top of his head, the first rays of sunshine were now felt instantly and were a warning to get out a hat or risk serious damage. Shaving was also more of a task, as his bristles had taken on the texture of carbon fibre and moisturiser had become a daily routine to keep his fair skin in better condition than many men of his age. Thankfully, his steel blue eyes, his most striking feature, had remained sharp, and he had no need for glasses, yet.

Standing down from Parliament in the UK caught many of his friends and family by surprise. Even those close to John were taken aback when he announced, the previous summer, that he would not be defending his massive Parliamentary majority in what was now described as one of the few safe seats his party had.

At that time nobody could have predicted that

the following year his party would return to
Government for the first time in nearly 100 years.
Even the prospect of being a Minister did not
make him regret for one moment his decision.
He knew the time was right to leave the House
of Commons. Westminster now felt a million
miles away. Parliament was now in session. His
successor would be commuting to London, while
he started to completely relax for the first time
in decades. He had added, *I'm Feeling Good*, to his
iPod, and he did.

After 30 years of campaigning on local, national,
and international issues, while he still had good
health, felt fit and had the drive to start something
new, John knew that it was either stay at
Westminster until retirement or make the change
– now. He had been in this situation before, when
working in the family construction business. He
realised that the thriving business only needed
one boss and when he told his father that he was
planning to move on, they both agreed that he
was the only family member with the ability and
drive to develop the company. An alternative plan
was worked out, for his father to retire early. John
bought the family business.

After another term in office, he would be
approaching 60. It would be too late for him to
start something new and in the back of his mind
was the memory that neither of his parents had

15

lived long enough to see their retirement.

He was not going to do the same. He had safely handed on his seat to his successor and felt content knowing that he would now have to work hard to rebuild the size of the majority John had left behind. As an empty nester, there was a new sense of freedom, and the daily routine of Westminster was not something he wanted to continue any longer. Like many theatrical performances, it looked more impressive from a distance, but when seen close up, the cracks in the grease paint were clear - and he was not too impressed by what went on. The time was right to move on. For the first time in years, he felt completely free.

Of the many plans he had for the future, one was to write down some of the stories, of events that had happened in his life, places he had been, people he had met and - not to publish a book, but to print a few copies and to leave a record for his grandchildren of what "Papa", as they called him, had done in his life. They were too young to understand this now, but the day would come when they would ask questions that nobody could answer. He wanted to write down his memories for them. Maria was aged six and Hope was two. They were the best thing that had happened to him, and one of the reasons he knew the time was right to step down from Parliament was to enjoy them as they grew up.

Some friends had suggested that standing for re-election one more time and then coasting through his final term would give him time to do this, but the only way he could do the job of an MP was the way he had always done it. This involved effectively being on the job seven days a week. He felt that even if the media, or some of his constituents, might not appreciate it, he could do no less for them and he loved almost every aspect of the job, he loved it too much to do a bad job of it.

While Hope was only two years old, she was already leaving her older sister behind in many ways. She could run, talk, play, like any other two-year-old. Maria's life was completely different and would be a constant struggle. Following a straightforward pregnancy, his daughter Sarah was assured all would be well and that there was no need to cancel the planned holiday to Greece to see her now extended family. While she had two first cousins in the UK, George, her husband, had fifty-six and many lived on the island. The holiday turned into a nightmare. Maria arrived two months early and at birth suffered a bleed in the brain. Cerebral palsy and epilepsy would make every day and night in her life a battle for survival. Constant visits to the hospital, daily medication, and a struggle to sleep every night for Maria, reminded

John daily of why he had never complained about his own life, and never would, for as long as she lived.

When constituents and others complained about how tough their life was, it took all his diplomatic skills to listen patiently and help where he could. Now, he would have much more time to enjoy the two new lights in his life. For all his enmity towards the Conservative party at Westminster, he always had an understanding of what life had been like at home for their leader in a way that few other MPs could have done. When the Prime Minister's son, who suffered from cerebral palsy and epilepsy too, slipped away, John was painfully aware that even such a short, troubled life could bring joy to everyone who had been lucky enough to be part of it. While Maria could not walk, she could talk, and together they would enjoy whatever time they might have.

Having written speeches for many years, participated in debates, researched topics that opened up new worlds to him, and produced articles for newspapers, magazines, and other publications – he thought that writing for his enjoyment should be a breeze. Gap years had not really been the norm when he had left school, and this was now his chance to take the gap year he felt was long overdue.

Now that the election was over, his office wound up and all the staff transferred to his successor, this was the time to take stock and plan for the future.

The last 20 years had left little time to read for pleasure or to write for enjoyment. Select Committee reports, briefings from lobby groups, research for Parliamentary debates, emails and correspondence, meetings, and campaigning, had consumed his life. He did not know how long it would take, but he knew there would be a withdrawal period from his old life. The one thing he always missed from his pre-MP days was the time he had for friends at home and abroad. A prolific long-letter writer, he had now become a short email writer and he now knew the time was right for a change.

Watching Prime Minister's Question Time or coverage of current affairs in the media could now be done as and when it suited. He was a political junkie but was surprised at how quickly he could do without his daily fix. He soon felt no need to waken up listening to the Today programme on the radio, pretending that this was everyone else's programme of choice too. He could listen to the headlines and then turn it off. He also developed a more critical eye for what he saw, either on the news or in Parliament. The staged events, the planted questions, the political opportunism of all parties made him wince. What had been the expected behaviour from the opposition was now being practiced against his party and it was not a pretty sight. Politicians of all parties willing to accept credit for things they were only loosely involved with, while dishing out the blame, or the dirt, even when there was little, or no fault involved on any side, was another aspect of political life he was glad to leave behind.

The country had been left in financial turmoil by the previous government, yet they now behaved as if the current problems had nothing to do with them and as if it was all the fault of the new Government. He smiled as he thought of the Liverpool taxi driver who told him, "If someone is sick in my cab, I don't blame the woman with the mop cleaning it up, for the mess that's been left there." He also knew that the new coalition was going to have a tough time from many who would feel let down by his Party, who could no longer enjoy being on the moral high ground of opposition and were now in the mire of Government. Watching colleagues sitting on the same benches as some individuals he could not personally stand also made it much easier to leave it all behind.

As the day started to warm up, the warmth felt as if it penetrated his bones. He felt the same feeling he had many years ago while driving through California. Carol was in Africa working and he had decided to go and drive down Highways 1 and 101 from San Francisco to San Diego and to catch up with some long-lost friends on the way. Visiting the magnificent Yosemite National Park, wine tasting in the Napa Valley and relaxing with friends, while listening to live music in the coastal towns of Encinitas and Carlsbad – it was his perfect life. Had he been able to surf, he thought, he might have wanted to stay there forever.

He was now experiencing a tranquillity not experienced for well over two decades and a feeling of freedom from a range of responsibilities. When he was in California, he had to return to earn a living and to be at home with his wife Carol and family. Now, the property portfolio he had built up over the years working in the family construction business provided more than enough income to get by on, and he could stay where he wanted, for as long as he liked.

To have a house available on a Greek island with none of the dodgy plumbing that was still all too common on the more remote islands, was an added bonus. The house had started as a pencil sketch on his drawing board in his Edinburgh home ten years before and then developed into a grand design; based on experience, life, dreams, and part of the house his parents had built, half a century ago in Tasmania.

John had remembered his mother saying that having a utility room for washing and drying, separate from the kitchen, was one of the best features of their home in Hobart. John kept a small piece of their original plans framed on his office wall and looked at it most days, wondering what their life had been like all those years ago.

His parents, Elsa and Andrew, had bought a plot of land and built their house just on the outskirts of Hobart in the 1950s, after they left Scotland and landed as £10 Poms in Australia. They moved to Tasmania to get married and to start their new life and family, on a small island thousands of miles away from home.

History repeated itself when John and Carol's only daughter Sarah fell in love with George on an even smaller island in Greece, fifty years later. Their holiday romance blossomed and after many trips back and forth from Scotland to Greece, and after meeting many members of both families, their wedding took place on Kalymnos.

With a plot of land as an advance wedding present from mum and dad, John used his old skills from many years before and produced the design and

Campaign Headquarters.

drawings for their new home. Sarah and George turned the grand design into reality over the next two years.

They moved in on their wedding day.

But their plans for the future were turned upside down by unexpected events. Sarah and George had moved to Scotland so that Maria could get the medical attention she required, and the house was now empty and in need of some company. It was the perfect location to capture the memories of the last decade and more.

As he opened a cool beer and looked into the distance, out over the port of Pothia, more recent memories of being on the island and the Big Wet Greek Wedding drifted into his mind.

Chapter 2
My Big Wet Greek Wedding

"What exactly is the deal with this wedding? John asked Sarah, sounding serious, but with a smile that said that he was not about to drive a hard bargain.

"Well dad... the wedding will be next September. We will have to have a reception for about three hundred people, after the engagement on the Friday, as everyone can't get into the club we have booked for the wedding reception on the Sunday. You see, the engagement happens at our house on the Friday, two days before the wedding. The priest comes, we exchange rings, you need to buy gold for George's parents, they will buy gold for you and lots of traditional things happen. There's music, my wedding dress is laid out on the bed, money is thrown on the bed, and babies are thrown on the bed to predict what sex our first child will be. Then we all go down to Therma, the little harbour just outside Pothia, for a party, music, Greek dancing, and it will go on late. George's brother Nick runs the taverna at Therma, so we will get a good deal. Then on the Sunday after that we have the wedding in the Greek Orthodox Church in Pothia, with three priests, we will have an outdoor reception on the cliff-top at Kasteli, the best club on the island, but we have to restrict the numbers to two hundred and fifty, as that's all they can handle, what with everything happening outdoors." Sarah stopped for breath and waited for her father's response.

Sarah was always bursting with energy and spoke at twenty to the dozen. She always had a happy smile on her face and along with her golden hair, her deep blue eyes melted her father's heart every time he looked at her.

"I assume that you'd like me to pick up the tab for these events? The reception will be like a normal wedding? At Therma is it a welcome drink for everyone and then nibbles? What if it rains on Sunday?"

"No dad, the tradition at the engagement is that everyone just drinks as much as they like, all night, and then they have a full meal and there is a band, more dancing, and more drink... then you pick up the tab... and it has not rained on the island in September in living memory"

"This is on top of the main wedding reception?"

"It's the tradition on the island... dad."

"I hear the tradition on the island is for the father of the bride to hand over his house to his daughter and her new husband on her wedding day as a wedding gift, but that's not happening either - unless you want to take on my mortgage and find me a new home as well. This feels like daylight robbery," he tried to sound worried, but his face said otherwise.

"Daaaaad," Sarah's blue eyes once again melted her father's heart the way they had done for the last twenty-one years. He was a willing victim to this "daylight robbery." It was a crime of passion, he thought to himself.

"It's a deal then." He knew inside that he and Carol would give her the wedding she wanted.

With only one child, he thought that it would probably still be much less expensive than a full-blown wedding in the UK and with only one daughter; the money was not the big issue. The fact that she was in love and marrying someone who felt the same way, was all that mattered.

The tradition of parents handing over their homes to the daughter on the wedding day still happened in about half of the marriages on Kalymnos but was something that was unlikely to catch on back home. Then he thought to himself that if he had been given his mother-in-law's large four bed-roomed detached house on Corstorphine Hill in Edinburgh, he might have had a different view of things.

The sound of the traditional Greek fiddles could be heard in the distance along with the marching of feet on cobblestones.

In the front garden of Sarah's new house, her father and all the Scots, clad in kilts, were feeling the heat and had consumed a few refreshments to cool down in preparation for the evening ahead. Mark, a tall, bearded bear of a man from the States, who had been invited with his girlfriend at the time, Sue, but who had arrived with his new squeeze, Christy, was the first to sound the alarm.

"We are about to be attacked by the Greeks," he shouted, as he saw the column approach from the distance. They were walking in time, like a precision machine; national service was still compulsory in Greece, and it showed. Men and women, young and old, with a glum look on every face and steely determination in every eye.

"It just like in Zulu," shouted Neil, a big fan of the movie and never slow to find a reference point from the film.

"Form up in three lines," barked John, "those drinking shorts in the front, good-looking ones in the middle and those without kilts to the rear. An orderly retreat, one drink, then fall back, one line at a time. Hold steady lads"

The advancing Greek family could see something they could not quite understand and thought it must be some old Scottish tradition. Men and women, young and old, liked the look of the men in "skirts" and the locals were looking forward to watching them in action, on the big day and dancing through the night.

"Sing men of Harlech" cried Neil, "it worked in Zulu," but this was a bridge too far, as nobody, not even Neil, had the faintest idea of the words. The Greek hordes advanced to the front door, the Scots retired to the kitchen bar, George and Sarah welcomed the guests to their home and the engagement party was underway.

"We don't send invitations to family events; everyone just knows to come. It is a small island, so word just gets round. People on neighbouring islands get a visit and an invitation, it's the tradition." Sarah explained.

"That will be why there are about a hundred and fifty people here, about fifty more than can get in the house and a hundred more than can hear what the priest is saying." John replied and accepted that this was a script he had no influence in

31

writing.

The visitors soon realised that there was little need to get close to the engagement service, as it was all in Greek, and, with the exception of Sarah, who was now fluent in the language, none of her family or friends understood a word. As long as Iain and his video camera were in the room, they might see it on the video later, with or without subtitles.

The wedding dress was laid out on the bed and money was thrown onto it, in the Greek tradition. Then a young child, a boy, flew through the air.

"No health and safety here" quipped Ewan, John's former right-hand man in the constituency.

As he was saying this, another baby, a girl, also flew through the air and landed on the bed.

"You are going to have a boy and a girl," said one of the many aunts, all called Maria.

John was wondering what would happen if one of them peed on the new gleaming white dress two days before the wedding. It's probably a tradition, he thought.

The house was getting hotter and hotter, and then John and Carol were invited into the room for the presentation of gold to their new extended family.

Sarah had organised it all; and rings, necklaces and bangles were placed on various people by unknown others. At least she appeared to know what was happening as she quickly got out of the way a split second before the tall bearded Greek Orthodox priest, waving a wet shrub in all directions, left most of the visitors drenched with holy water.

Everyone from the house, and many more, made their own way to the taverna by a small beach at Therma and it was the perfect location for a night out. Just outside the main town of Pothia and by the water's edge, the harbour lights were sparkling in the distance and the evening ferries were a busy backdrop to the party. The cool breeze of the evening, the gentle Greek music and the welcome from the new family made it feel like a scene from a movie.

A voice in the dark sounded out, "Mamma Mia, was just like this, a wedding on a Greek island, and nobody here is sure who the bride's father is either"

Just then the music burst into life and Sarah and George leapt onto one of the central tables and started a new dance. Sarah dazzled the audience with her smile and personality, while George and Sarah's dancing ability impressed everyone. After the demonstration, they leapt onto the ground and made sure everyone joined in. All the dances had a similar style and before long every visitor felt they should be on the Greek version of Strictly Come Dancing.

The evening was the perfect first experience of Greek hospitality for most of the guests.

Some had been to Greece before, but not one had enjoyed it like this. By the time the evening was over, and the music had stopped, it felt like they had all been at the wedding already, and it was still two days away.

Getting to Kalymnos involved flying to the island of Kos and then taking a ferry from the port of Mastahari to Pothia, the main town on the island. Most guests came from the UK this way, but Mark and Christy flew from LA to London to Athens to Kos. Fos and Carolyn decided to sail around the Greek islands and arrive in time for the engagement party. Their absence at the engagement party was noticed, but nobody worried, as Fos's timekeeping on dry land was not great, so most people expected him to be still at sea and to see them at some time in the days ahead. They arrived safe and well on the Saturday and immediately set out to explore the excellent scuba diving at Telendos, a smaller island to the west of Kalymnos, separated 400 years ago by an earthquake. The ruins of old towns were within scuba diving depth.

Unfortunately, on Fos's first dive an octopus was attracted by the dark band in the middle of his shorts and decided that it looked like a place of safety. It wrapped itself around his shorts and would not let go. Fos's concern was that its beak would decide to nip him just where he would feel it most.

Lynn, Sarah's godmother, and her husband Niall were making a family holiday of it. Their three children would be bridesmaids and a pageboy, and, on the Saturday, they decided to explore the island by taxi.

"Head for taxi square, it's just behind the main street, you can't miss it, and agree on a price before you start," the manager of the Olympic Hotel had instructed them that morning.

Having found one taxi cheaper than the rest, they jumped in and headed along the cliff-top road to Massouri, where there were beaches for the kids.

"Bloody hell, that was close," screamed Lynn as the cab lurched towards the cliff edge and then back again.

"He's only got one arm!" whispered Niall. "Well, he has only got one that works, the other is in a cast, it's broken, and he has a manual gearbox. When he changes gear, he has no hands on the wheel... we are on the road to hell."

"Don't panic," thought Lynn, keep calm, shouting will only make it worse.

"The children are car-sick, can you slow down," she said slowly. Speaking with a Greek accent, hoping this would help the driver understand.

"Nai," answered the driver, it meant yes in Greek, but sounded like no in English.

They panicked and started to shout at him. He thought they were complaining that he was going too slowly. He decided to speed up, changing gear rapidly, with no hands on the wheel. His knees were steering the cab, their lives were flashing before them all as they huddled in the back. Just then his mobile phone started to ring.

They caught the local bus back to Pothia at the end of the day and hired a car the following morning to get to the wedding.

Another hot sunny Sunday morning. The perfect day for a wedding, and a reception overlooking the Aegean Sea, with a multitude of small islands in the distance. If it was to be like Friday or Saturday night, it would be a warm moonlit night after an extremely hot day. A breeze up the kilt would be most welcome for all those in full Highland dress.

Unlike church weddings in the UK, or Greek ones on television, where the father marches his daughter down the aisle, the parents, bride and groom all meet up outside the church, where the bride and groom enter together. Getting to the church is done quite separately. The groom's family quietly make their way there with no fuss, while the bride and her family march from their new home, through the village or town in a great procession.

"When are the buses arriving?" enquired John.

"They will be here in plenty of time, George has arranged everything," insisted Sarah.

"Looks like another great day, although it looks like rain clouds are gathering in the distance, stormy weather ahead" joked her dad.

"One bus has broken down; you will need to go in two separate groups to the starting point for the march through the village. The one bus that's coming is late, so you will have to leave the moment it arrives. Then it will come back and pick up the second group. It will drop everyone at the same point, and then you will all march to the church. The band will meet you there and they know where to go, just follow them. I must go, I shouldn't be here, I am not supposed to see Sarah before the wedding, it's bad luck." George flew out the door, heading for the church and to try to calm his parents down.

The procession through the village was led by a band of Greek musicians and every house balcony was full of people out to see the men in skirts. John and Carol were on either side of Sarah – it was her perfect day. The full Highland dress was going down a storm and the extra weight was worth carrying for the effect it had on the day.

One thing which baffled John was that one young attractive girl in the march was carrying a tray with a large glass of wine on it. Underneath the tray was a cloth which had the uncanny appearance of a huge pair of pants. Another tradition, he smiled to himself and thought. Nothing would faze him today.

Arriving at the church, both families met, and Sarah and George were suddenly together and at the heart of everything. Iain and his video camera kept appearing in different places to get good shots as his creative juices were clearly beginning to flow. It was only when he had managed to get into a high-level pulpit and nearly dislodged a stone dove, which almost came crashing down on the gathering, that John signalled for him to ease up.

The wedding service was intense, traditional, and once again a complete mystery to the visitors, but at the centre of it all was the most beautiful image of his daughter bathed in candlelight.

On the island, the traditional way of celebrating important events is to throw sticks of dynamite, in the way that people use fireworks elsewhere. It was no great surprise then to hear explosions just as the wedding ceremony was coming to an end and most visitors thought it must be the normal way to mark the event. But there were also strange noises coming from outside the door of the church and it sounded as if all was not well. The skies outside suddenly darkened, and lightning lit up the sky. Roars of thunder followed, and the heavens opened.

The mystery of the high kerb stones was answered, as the road outside turned into a fast-flowing river. Lightning struck again and the church was plunged into darkness, apart from a number of candles, which had been lit earlier in the service.

The bus arrived to take the first group of guests to the reception, it left in a hurry. As George went to find out what was happening, Sarah was standing on her own, in the middle of a candlelit Greek orthodox church in a country thousands of miles from home, looking like an angel.

The lightning had struck the only power station on the island; there had been a flash flood and landslides on the cliff-top road. The venue for the reception had been washed out but nobody, especially the visitors, had any idea of this. The bus, which had left the church with the first group of visiting guests, was now stuck outside the club at Kasteli, with no way back to town, as the blocked coastal road was the only way back to Pothia. The driver had left the bus to find out what was going on and had locked the door to stop the passengers from wandering off. They felt trapped in a Turkish bath - which was getting hotter and hotter.

The music playing, Zorba's dance was on a loop and driving them mad. Help, was being written on the bus windows, in reverse, in the condensation. Gordon, with a heart condition, was a major worry as his wife loosened his tie and fanned his flushed face. The bus door opened, the heat rushed out, the rain washed in, and the driver announced something, in great detail, then jumped into the driver's seat to light up a cigarette. Unfortunately, nobody understood a word he said.

Sarah was still standing in the church being assured that it was a good sign and that with all this rain, this year there would be a bumper olive crop. The rain had followed the Scots to Kalymnos; it was a good omen they said. She could not quite see it that way.

As the rain poured down the staff at harbour-side restaurants could only look on as chairs and tables were washed out to sea. The locals quickly adapted to the unfolding circumstances. All restaurants with wood-burning ovens were soon full, temporary lighting was set up, live music continued and the guests from the wedding soon found alternative places to eat and to spend the evening. The only thing missing from the party was the bride and groom.

Once the word that the reception had been cancelled had spread, the locals vanished, but the visitors continued in a party mood, with a number of mini receptions being held at tavernas and hotels around the harbour. The bus had now made it back using back roads and a wartime spirit prevailed. It was a wedding night like no other.

After making sure that everyone was safe and well, the bride and groom returned to their new home to spend their wedding night together and to think about planning the reception – again.

After a very late night, it was a slow start the next day. George travelled to every hotel and apartment block where guests were staying, to let everyone know that the reception would be held the next day, at the same venue, but moved inside - just in case.

Same-day dry cleaners saved the day; dresses, shirts and other once-used wedding outfits were brought back to life again, for round two on Monday evening.

On what would have been the perfect evening for an outdoor Mediterranean wedding at a cliff-top venue overlooking moonlit islands in the Aegean Sea, two hundred and fifty members of the now extended Greek family enjoyed dancing the Gay Gordons with the men in full Highland dress.

John could not resist adding to his father-of-the-bride speech, that as well many people from Scotland arriving in Kalymnos for the wedding, they had also brought the Scottish weather.

What he decided not to say was that he was also delighted, and relieved, that he was not following

43

one local tradition - where the bride's father handed over his house to the newlyweds.

Chapter 3
Tough Times

Life on the island had changed much since John and Carol had made their first visit to Kalymnos. Back then it was vibrant and full of life, with tour companies filling hotels and apartments throughout the summer season. Restaurants had few empty tables, and the clubs and bars were full, with locals and visitors drinking and dancing until the wee small hours. Since then, much had changed.

The economic downturn experienced by much of Europe and America had hit Greece and the Greek islands particularly badly. Many tour companies had pulled out from more difficult to get to places and islands, such as Kalymnos, and tourists to the Dodecanese islands in the south-eastern Aegean Sea often only went as far as Kos, which benefited from direct flights from many UK airports. This avoided the extra costs and risks involved in connecting with a small ferry to the smaller islands, which had a small airport but no direct flights from mainland Europe. Local tourist information for the region was also centred in the main town on the island of Kos and they were now much less likely to direct tourists to the outlying small islands of Leros, Pserimos and Kalymnos when their own hotels had many empty beds to fill. Many small shops and second homes were now boarded up all year round and some villages on Kalymnos now looked like ghost towns, even in the summer, as well as in the winter months.

Greece was particularly badly placed to deal with the economic crisis sweeping through many economies for a variety of reasons. Before joining the Euro, its government had increased public sector salaries and taken on large debts to finance the Olympic Games and other expenditures, while failing to reform its pension system and the method of collecting taxes. It was unable to fund many of its promises in the good times; in the bad times, it was a disaster waiting to happen, and it did.

Nationally and locally, there was a history of corruption as well as tax evasion. People were often employed, not because of their ability to do the job, but because of who they knew, what contacts their families had built up, or to repay favours. Those most likely to avoid taxes were not the usual suspects in the building trade or in restaurants, but those in the medical profession and the media. Doctors in Athens regularly declared low incomes in order to pay little tax but were usually wealthy enough to run Mercedes and BMW cars parked in the hospital car parks. While the country struggled to pay its way, the number of yachts in Pireaus harbour continued to grow year after year. The sums just did not add up. The economy was in no shape to join a currency union with other much stronger countries such as France and the efficient German economy. When it did, the cracks soon began to show and the impact on Kalymnos unfolded as quickly as it did in Athens.

Unemployment increased while tourism reduced and casual work became hard to obtain. The brightest and best young people for some years have left the island to attend universities elsewhere, now many others were also leaving to find better-paid work abroad and to support their families on the island. Sarah and George, who had now settled in Scotland, regularly sent help to his family on the island, clothes for the children and other essentials all now increasing in price. The rate of inflation was rising and the income of many was falling. The island was heading into its own mini-economic crisis, ahead of the rest of Greece.

Walking around Kalymnos, John could see the problems mounting as each week went by. He was observing and soaking up many aspects of local life. Neither a local nor a tourist, he felt like a Flaneur, a description he was once given to him by a French waitress in an Edinburgh café.

Much of the island not only looked a mess and run down, but the locals also looked run down, worn out and depressed. Many men hung around cafes all day, looking as if they had given up all hope. The women had to make do with what little resources they had, and some went hungry to make sure their children were fed regularly. It was a long way from the situation John had witnessed first-hand in Africa when he used to visit many countries receiving overseas aid from the UK, to help with food supply, clean drinking water and the fight against many diseases. He thought that although it might not be Africa, it was halfway there. It felt a million miles away from the comfort and security of the UK.

One mistake people often make when they see images of Africa is that they think there is no food available, when often there is plenty of food, there is just no money to buy it. It was the same in Kalymnos, as the shops were full, and many simply had no money to go to the shops, to buy what they wanted or needed. The islanders were also now suffering because many had built up personal debt, or credit, at many shops and businesses and while the future was brighter, and this was just the normal way of life, these amounts were treated as "money in the bank." People would pay their debts one day and all would be well. Now that future was no longer so certain and for the first time in many years, people became aware that if these debts were not to be cleared, they could not pay off their own debts. The prospect of a downward spiral of a recession was looming large in the minds of many.

The history of the island was a long and proud one. The ancient relics from a bygone age were still to be found by locals, who would often try to sell them on the black market, risking prison sentences for the chance to get ready cash from an anonymous buyer, rather than hand them to the museum and receive a much smaller finder's reward. This would have also allowed locals and tourists to enjoy the artefacts and could have provided another attraction for visitors, but personal greed and ready cash often won out over the common good. This was another wasted opportunity, where a quick profit had taken the place of a long-term sustainable future. So much was wrong on the island, and little was being done to change anything.

John felt a growing frustration at the part the local people were playing in their own downfall. It reminded him of his time at Westminster when discussions were taking place about how many billions of pounds each party would promise the NHS to cope with the ever-growing demand. While every party tried to outbid the others, nobody was prepared to listen to his, and others' arguments about reducing the demand for it.

If only people would cut out smoking, drink less alcohol, take more exercise, cut down their sugar intake, and live a more healthy lifestyle, in some areas of healthcare this could save millions. "It's not rocket science," he would say. We cannot avoid getting older, but we can avoid becoming obese, we can reduce the incidence of many cancers, he would often say. At that time he was unaware of how he would see this close up in the years to come.

He believed the problem was that people wanted to behave as they liked and then look to others, usually politicians, to deal with the consequences or solve their problems.

He smiled when he thought back to some of the odder requests his constituents had asked him to deal with as their MP. Such as the woman who had been convinced her neighbour had stolen her cat and who wanted John to get it back. Sounding to John that this constituent was in fact feeding someone else's cat, he asked, "who pays the vet's bills for the cat?" On discovering it was the neighbour who did this, feeling like he had cracked the cat ownership problem, he declared, "It's her cat."

Promoting personal responsibility was never a vote-winner for any party. In fact, it was often a vote loser. The party which reminded people that as many people were living longer, they would not only have to work for longer before getting a state pension but would also have to pay more into their pension scheme to cover a longer retirement, was not a party people wanted to vote for. While the political party promising higher pensions and a reduction in retirement age or lower taxes, was the one people would support. He was aware that one problem with democracy was that many politicians were elected because they had promised to deliver what the electorate did not actually want to pay for. The problems were exactly the same in Greece.

The good money made in Kalymnos during the era when sponge fishing supported many families was now over and tourism was what kept the island alive. It was one of the relatively unspoilt islands of the Dodecanese in the south-eastern Aegean Sea, without the overdevelopment suffered by many others, and rock-climbing had added an extra appeal, which also extended the tourist season. It was not a pretty island, but the lure of a simpler life, without the high-rise hotels and tourist crowds was exactly what appealed to many and was the reason he first visited Kalymnos a decade before. He could not have guessed back then the impact it would have on his life.

As he wandered around the island on his daily walk, he was impressed by some of the larger houses and the quality of the build. Sarah and George had not only managed to build a substantial home, but the quality of the finish, the marble flooring, the ceramic tiles, and the hand-made kitchen were all as good as anything found in Edinburgh or London. While some large new houses were occupied, many had been built by those who had made their fortunes abroad and who planned to return to retire on the island and many were empty for much of the year, contributing nothing to the economy, not even the employment of cleaners, gardeners, or caretakers.

Local resentment was also growing towards immigrants, as it often does during tough times. Local and national politicians were also being blamed for the way life was now unfolding.

Many of the elderly and those who had retired early were fearful that their fourteen monthly pension payments from the Government every year were at risk and many of the young unemployed were growing in their anger towards those migrants who had arrived from Albania or Turkey and who often did the most menial jobs that the Greeks considered beneath them, but who were now being blamed for stealing their jobs.

One of the most flagrant abusers of his position was the Mayor of the island, who not only received a good salary for running what was the equivalent size of a single council ward back in

Scotland, but who had also managed to employ many members of his family in plum jobs on the island council, including his cousin as his own personal driver, or chauffeur. The word was that he had also included his extensive group of employed relatives in the council's private medical insurance scheme and he was often brazen enough to charge meals at various restaurants to his expense account. Nobody wanted to rock the boat about this, just in case he made life difficult for them.

The island council under his control not only dealt with education but also the utilities and could also cut off water and electricity supplies to those who owed it money. Being Mayor of Kalymnos was not only a lucrative post, it was also a position of power and controlled many aspects of life on the island. He was not someone anybody wanted to cross.

Giving advice and helping others had been a way of life for 30 years, but John had now put on his blinkers in order to move on from elected office. No longer would he spend hours working late into the night on correspondence and working to develop solutions to problems on behalf of others, only to find that they would go and do their own thing, regardless of his advice. No longer would he continue with a variety of responsibilities in the community, as many people had hoped he would still do, after stepping down. He had given over 30 years of his life to public service and the time for changing down a gear had arrived. It might not be easy to move on, but he was determined to do so.

He had decided to choose one or two charitable causes he wanted to support and to give his time, energy or money to no others, with the exception of the odd beggar on the street, and he had decided that after his return to Scotland he would keep more of his time free to enjoy his grandchildren, his family and friends, to travel, to read more, play his guitar, look after his garden and, for the first time in his life, to relax. In the meantime, he would get on with writing the story of his life.

Chapter 4
Looking Back

Prizing open one of the unopened tea chests containing old papers from his grandparents' house, for the first time in his life John was able to uncover the history of his German grandfather Werner and his wife, Rose.

Throughout John's life, he had been aware that his grandfather had come over from Germany as a young man in his twenties and that the family home and business had been lost to the Communist regime when Germany was partitioned after World War II. He had no idea what the family home looked like, or what exactly his family's hometown was like until he removed the lid from that box.

It contained diaries, letters and photographs going back to the birth of his grandfather on 4th March 1902 in the village of Thale, close to the Harz Mountains. Family photos were not only in perfect condition but also annotated with the names and dates of those in the pictures. It was clear where his family lived and what the home and family saw-mill and timber business were like. A 1902 photograph of the workforce outside the timber mill in Quedlinburg and the parquetry flooring workshop said more than words ever could.

The mill had originally been powered by water, directed along a mill lade to a water turbine and from there, belts had driven the workshops and powered the entire business. Saws, spindles, drills, and other machinery had all been water-powered. Photographs of a teenage Werner as a schoolboy, working in the fields during World War I, letters explaining his move to Amsterdam between the wars, where he worked in the office of a toy company and his journey to Edinburgh, where he met and fell in love with Rose Tinney. More love letters detailing their romance and marriage, without the blessing of his family. Returning to Germany, with a wife and young son, Harold, and typewritten application letters to the UK Home Office, Aliens Branch, to apply for permanent residency in the UK. Settling in Edinburgh, then when war breaks out, being detained by the authorities, as were many others of German extraction. Letters detailing the struggle of surviving during the war and then the birth of two more daughters, Elizabeth, and Sylvia. Post-war letters and more diaries. Everything catalogued with Teutonic precision.

Of all the letters and documents, two made an immediate impression on John. One was a note from Werner to Rose asking her out on a date. It gave the location, Orwell Terrace, near Haymarket in Edinburgh and the time to meet as 7.30 pm. It also gave the end time of the date as 10.30 pm.

Never a good way to impress a girl, he thought, saying in advance when her time was up. The other was a government leaflet advising what to do in the event of a Nazi invasion. The graphic was a large jack-boot with a spur in the shape of a swastika. Clever graphics to get a message across, he thought, even back then. John understood the effectiveness of good graphics on any literature. He had written, designed and used literature to good effect for decades.

John went straight to the diary for 1954, and the date of his birth, the 11th of February – nothing. The 12th of February – nothing. Then 13th February – bingo.

The diary entry read, *"Today we received a telegram from Elsa in Australia, saying that she had given birth to a baby boy on the 11th of February, and that Elsa and her new baby were both well. Andrew and Elsa had decided to call him John, and he is a lovely smiling baby. A letter with all the news is in the post."*

Delving into the letters folder, there it was, a letter from his mother to her parents, telling them about his birth. John sat and stared at it for a while.

For many years he rarely shed a tear, but he had become more emotional in his later years and a sad film could now be responsible for a few tears running down his cheek. He had a feeling this was about to be one of those tear-jerking moments, and he was right.

Dear Mother and Father,

Hopefully, you will have received my telegram to let you know that we now have a brother for David. He was 7lbs 8oz and is the most beautiful baby in the world. We have called him John and I am so happy. To be honest, he is much better looking than his older brother. This may be because I am able to breastfeed him and while I tried to with David, it was just not possible. All being well, one day, before too long, you will be able to see him in the flesh.

Now that your plans to migrate to Australia with Sylvia and Harold have fallen apart, we have decided to return to Scotland, and as soon as the house Andrew is building is complete, we will put it on the market. Although it will be sad to leave our new home, we are looking forward to bringing our entire family back home to Scotland.

At present we are thinking about travelling to Canada, after a long holiday in Scotland, but who knows what the future might bring?

The sale of the house should pay off all our debts, buy our return tickets and leave us with enough to last for a while - before Andrew has to start working again. We might just choose to have a fresh start again in

Scotland.

I will be in hospital for 10 days, which is normal here, and after I return home I will write again, as soon as we have more information about our future plans.

Sorry for this being such a short letter, but my new baby needs fed again.

Lots of Love,

Elsa

John was stunned. This letter from his late mother, all the information about his family, photos, diaries and more had been lying in a cupboard in a house occupied by his Aunt Sylvia for the last 20 years, since his mother had died, and he had not even been aware it had existed.

He sat for a moment to take it all in. He would go through every document and every photograph, letter, and diary, to understand how life unfolded all those years ago.

Not knowing what was there, all that time, made him determined never to be in that same position with his own daughter or grandchildren. He would talk and listen to them so that they would know him. He also planned to write down what he could recall, so that they could read what happened in his life and most of all he vowed to savour every minute of their lives, however long or short that might be.

He thought briefly about his own life and his happy childhood as one of four brothers living in Carrick Knowe, Edinburgh, attending his first school, Carrick Knowe Primary, where his passion was football. John always found schoolwork relatively easy, but what he enjoyed most was playing football with his friends, before school started in the morning, at lunchtime and after school in the local park, until teatime.

Then on to Forrester High School, where he still found schoolwork quite easy and again was often near to the top of the class, but he did work hard when it came to exam times in his fourth, fifth and sixth years, as he still had no idea what to do for a career and enough exam passes would give him the option of going to university, if he wanted to. At school he continued to enjoy his football, but it was clear to him that others he would play against, Graham Souness and Paul Heggarty, who both played for Scotland in later years and Stevie Hancock who was the best of all, were of a much higher calibre than him. Being invited to a trial for the then mighty Partick Thistle Football Club was the highlight of his playing days. Being told he would not be signed up came not long after John had given up any aspirations to be a professional player and it was something he took in his stride. By then he had his Lambretta motor scooter, and he had found something to replace football as his number one interest– a girlfriend.

He could not have imagined that meeting Carol at a party when he was 17 would shape the rest of his life. Leaving school at 18 and moving on to Heriot Watt University to study Economics and Accountancy, as Carol went on from St George's Girls School to Edinburgh Art College. Then leaving University after one term, when he decided that he did not want to become either an accountant or economist. Later in life, he would see that others who failed to graduate included Woody Allen, Steve Jobs, Richard Branson, Bill Gates, Tom Hanks, and many others who had made a mark in life, so it was not the end of the world he convinced himself.

Joining the family building business as a temporary measure to help his mother and father, who needed a driver, as he had just lost his driving licence for a year, after being caught driving above the permitted alcohol level. Staying there twenty years and eventually buying a small share of the business each year until he owned the majority of shares, to allow his father to retire early and enjoy life.

Watching his father die at 65 after two years as a

"vegetable" following a massive stroke and taking him in a wheelchair to his mother's funeral, where he could only moan and wail. The sadness of it all left him with a knot in his stomach. Neither parent living long enough to reach retirement age in good health would be something that would play a key part in John's decision to move on from the family business and later to stand down from life as an MP, when nobody expected him to.

He knew that statistically the odds were not on his side for a long life in retirement and he was not going to put off until tomorrow what he could do today.

After the death of his parents, the family business was no more a family affair, and it was time to move on. Although they could get on his nerves, as parents often do, he felt lucky to have worked closely with both of them for many years, and he missed them every day. He was not only their son, he also looked after their financial affairs, and organised the purchase of their new house in the leafy suburbs of Edinburgh, which they both loved. He was one of four, but he was the one they could rely on to make sure all was well and that their future was secure. David was a lovable rogue, often in and out of trouble with the law. Stephen was a great storyteller, a good laugh and great company, but suffered from mood swings, which were a worry for his parents. Michael, a great Elvis fan, had grown from a fragile child to a strapping man and was dependable and considerate, but opted for redundancy and to get another salaried job elsewhere, rather than take the risks involved running the family business, when the offer was made to him by John.

At times, all four brothers had worked in the family business. David was a carpenter, Stephen was a plumber and Michael worked in the office and stores, but only John had what it took to run things, hire and fire men, work late evenings and weekends and be on call through the night when required. He borrowed from the bank to keep the business going. Three wanted to get paid a weekly wage and have their evenings and weekends off, and one took all the risks and worked late into the night.

He sold the business for next to nothing in order to keep all the employees in a job and to avoid them facing redundancy. It broke his heart when some years later the new owner turned to drink and let the entire business collapse. It would not be the only time in his life that he would see alcohol destroy a life.

Not selling the business premises and instead leasing it to the new owner proved to be a wise move in more ways than one. Along with some savings, renting the business premises to the new owner provided John with enough resources to survive for at least four years away from paid work and he decided to take the opportunity of going back to university. In the back of his mind, it was something he felt he had missed and would have enjoyed. Now, even with a wife and daughter, he had the chance to make a change in direction and return to university as a mature student. As he walked into his first class at Napier University, his new student colleagues assumed he was the lecturer and were surprised when he joined them and sat at the back.

No more economics and accountancy for him and a change to civil engineering would allow him to use the experience of working in and then running a building firm. It would also help him cope with a return to full-time studies and competition from younger sharper students, who had just left school and would now be ahead of him in the new world of computers and the developing world of the internet. He had grown up in a pre-computer age. However, a future as a civil engineer was not to be. After two years away from the construction industry, he decided never to return to it... ever, and after realising that he should work in a field he really enjoyed, transferred to a Video/TV and Radio production course at Telford College.

This proved to be a great move for him, as the combination of academic and practical work out in the field and in the studio was what he loved. After completing the course, he did a post-graduate summer school at Cornell University in New York State to develop his skills further.

He had explained to the course Professor that he only had a diploma and not a full degree but was accepted onto the course along with other graduates from the USA, Latin America, Morocco, and Europe. It was like being at the United Nations. When the course ended, he was asked to meet up with Professor running the summer school, Shohini Ghosh, for a chat. This was unusual as no others had been asked for such a meeting.

He thought that the lack of a degree might be an issue after all. It was much to his surprise that he was asked to return the following year to be a teaching assistant on the same course. Apparently, the entire faculty had been so impressed by his performance and positive attitude that they wanted him back, and this time he could bring his family and stay in the hall for visiting scholars. "Not bad for someone with no degree," he thought to himself.

He would use the intervening year to good effect and worked freelance with professional corporate video companies and produced his own work for causes he believed in. This included working on a BAFTA winning documentary, *This Mine is Ours*

with a master-craftsman director David Peat, and
going to Ukraine in the post-Chernobyl period
to look at the effect of the radiation on young
children who were dying in a Kiev hospital. He
also produced a fundraising video for use by the
Sick Kids Hospital in Edinburgh. Never thinking
he would ever have reason to visit it again. How
wrong he was.

After time gaining experience with a variety of
companies, he set up his new business, ABC
Productions Ltd. He enjoyed the move into
corporate video production and was based back at
his old building company premises in Haymarket.
Working with like-minded people on a freelance
basis, he no longer had the responsibilities of
employing staff, but had plenty of work he enjoyed
and the start of a new chapter in his story.

Throughout his life, John had been a natural
campaigner and he joined the Scottish Liberal
Party in 1980, not to get elected, but to help
locally and nationally to campaign "to improve the
neighbourhood first and then to change to world"
as he would say, when asked why he had joined a
party that nobody usually voted for and very few
ever joined.
He developed skills as a community campaigner

and was popular locally when residents had
to deal with authority or the city council. He
articulated solutions to local problems on behalf
of his neighbourhood and spearheaded the local
campaign to reduce the volume of dog shit in
the local park. His "Scoop That Poop" campaign
mobilised residents, the council, dog owners, the
media and more, ending up with dog-free zones in
the park and free scoops and waste bags available
at shops and libraries. For the first time, John's
face started to appear in the local papers as a man
who would get things done.

He enjoyed campaigning and was asked by the
Liberals to stand for election to the Edinburgh
Council in 1984, but at that time he was fully
committed to working in the family business and
at times, due to his father's health problems,
he was the boss. He was selected as a council
candidate but soon after had to stand down as
a candidate as once again his father's health left
John running the business. A good friend, Veronica
Crerar, an Edinburgh lawyer, stepped up and took
his place.

John organised everything in her campaign to
remove the sitting Conservative councillor in a
ward she had represented for many years. When
Veronica was elected, it became the first of many
successful election campaigns he would run. He
then organised successful elections every two

years for others, and then the local Liberal party
decided that when the local government was
reorganised in 1995 he should go for it himself,
and stand as a candidate.

There would be a new all-powerful Edinburgh
City Council replacing two previous councils
and after eleven years as a Councillor, Veronica
decided it was time to stand down. The wards and
responsibilities would be new, and it was time for
a new candidate. John was unanimously selected
by the members of his party to be their candidate
and when he won the South-East Corstorphine
ward with a massive majority, everyone was
delighted, and few were surprised. He then went
on to be re-elected with an even greater majority
four years later.

As a councillor and election agent, he
masterminded the victory over the Conservative
party in the 1997 General Election, to make
Edinburgh West a Liberal Democrat seat at
Westminster for the first time in living memory.
A surprise announcement by his newly elected
MP, Donald Gorrie, that he would only stand for
one term left John shocked and seeking a new
candidate for the next election. He approached
the leader of his council group, Jenny Dawe,
offering to be her election agent and campaign
organiser. It was a seat he was convinced his party
could hold on to, even with a new candidate, but

she enjoyed life on the Council and her other work in Edinburgh and did not want to be an MP. She suggested that John should go for it, which he did, and he was elected as the Member of Parliament for Edinburgh West at Westminster in June of 2001.

At the time of the election, there was a belief that life at Westminster would be quiet, possibly even dull, as the Scottish Parliament was now up and running, dealing with many domestic issues. John's main interests were national and international and at that time he, like many others, had no idea how foreign affairs would dominate the next decade. On September 11th that year John received a call from his Westminster assistant, Stephen, saying, "Turn on your TV, the world has stopped."

The twin towers in New York had just been attacked, 3,000 people were estimated to have died as the result of the largest-ever terrorist attack on the USA. The numbers 9/11 would have a new meaning to everyone on the planet for the rest of their lives.

Parliament was recalled and Westminster would see much of the next ten years dominated by the war in Iraq, Afghanistan, terrorism, and other problems in the Middle East.
The debate on going to war in Iraq was one of his proudest moments in Westminster, as he and the

Liberal Democrats stood up to a torrent of abuse from the Blair government, the Conservative opposition, and the media.

Under the leadership of Charles Kennedy, the Liberal Democrats were leading the opposition to the war in Iraq in Parliament. Outside Westminster, John marched on the streets along with a million others who opposed the war and inside Parliament he spoke out and challenged Tony Blair on the issue of Weapons of Mass Destruction.

He kept the video of Blair's answer to his question about WMD and watched it from time to time. He also remembered clearly how Blair's Government offered Saddam Hussein the opportunity to stay in power if he would give up his WMD and then how the justification for war evolved to regime change, when it was later proved by the weapons inspectors that no WMDs existed.

Blair lied to him then and he got away with murder, as John saw it. At the start of Prime Minister's Questions, the Prime Minister always listed the names of UK soldiers who had died in any week.

When John later asked the Prime Minister about the number of civilians who had also died, although it was estimated that the number exceeded 100,000, the reply was that the UK government did not count them.

John had met President Bashir of Sudan, who was wanted for crimes against humanity and war crimes in Darfur. John always believed Tony Blair and George Bush should have been charged with war crimes too.

Throughout all this time, from working in the family business, returning to studies, setting up a new business and being elected to the Council and then Parliament, Carol, was by his side. Married in 1975, while she was still at Edinburgh Art College, she visited Africa regularly and had become one of Scotland's best wildlife artists. They were joined in 1981 by their daughter Sarah, who, at age 16, had gone with them and three of her girlfriends on holiday to Kalymnos, where she met George.

His daily walk on the island, on small remote goat tracks along cliff-tops and over hilltops to areas no locals or even the few tourists rarely reached, allowed him to order his thoughts, and although his entire life was at times swimming around in his head, he now decided that it was time to stop looking back and to look forward. "Who knows what the future might bring?" he thought. He was often joined by a stray dog he nicknamed Bobby. Bobby would appear for a while, walk with him, and then vanish just as quickly. Whenever Bobby did not appear, John missed his company.

That evening he was in no mood for writing anything, and he headed to the north end of the island and the small village of Emporios, where he could enjoy a meal and a drink and play Yourgos, the café owner's, guitar as the cool evening breeze kept him awake. He played *Don't Think Twice It's Alright*. "Maybe a good title for my book, if Bob Dylan had not used it first." He pondered.

They sang and played until the sun rose the next morning. His thoughts were now becoming clear about what he needed to do. He was going to stay on the island, finish writing his story and do something about the state the island was in, then head home to Scotland.

Chapter 5
A Room With A View

A shower is for getting clean, a bath is for relaxing in... and for thinking.

When designing the house for Sarah, John was keen to incorporate an idea he had always wanted in his own home. A long cast iron bath, with a view through a clear glass window towards the distant countryside.

This had never been possible in the suburbs of Edinburgh, as apart from the lack of a country view, the neighbours would not have appreciated being able to see into his bathroom at any time of day. John also realised that the view in was not something he would inflict on anyone. This became very clear after he had upgraded his own bathroom and included a large mirror covering one entire wall of the bathroom, which looked great, until he realised that when he stood up in the bath, he would be faced with a full-frontal image of himself, not something he would ever want anyone outside to see.

The plot of ground purchased for the new house was set high on a hill overlooking the harbour of Pothia. The main town of Kalymnos was to the south, and looking north, from the back of the house, were three abandoned windmills, built many centuries ago. While the sails had gone, the large circular stone structures dominated the craggy landscape, along with their conical tops and sail mechanism, which had been partially reconstructed. Set against the backdrop of the distant hills and lit by the rising morning sun and golden light of the setting sun each evening, it was the perfect view from the rear of the new home. The positioning and height of the bath and window were set to maximise this natural advantage. The view was perfect, and although Sarah and George were not consulted about this design detail, both knew he was on to a winner, and they were happy to let him make one room exactly how he wanted to.

Soaking in a bath was where John did his best thinking. He would go into an almost semi-conscious state and drift off back in time, or into some fantasy of the future. He would invent things, sort out problems and make sure he had all his bases covered for whatever situation he thought might unfold. He would plan out his work and campaigns in great detail, and he developed a way of knowing what his opponents might think, in order to be one step ahead of them. He would look at all the opportunities, threats, dangers, weaknesses, and strengths of every course of action he could take on any issue. His ability to be one step ahead of the pack was not luck or by

accident, as many thought, it was by design, hard work, detailed preparation, and forward planning.

He could recall events from years ago in minute detail and this often surprised him, as he regularly forgot where he left his car keys or door keys five minutes before, but he could still remember many events from his past with great clarity, as if he was watching it now on television.

He thought back to when he attended an event in the Odeon cinema as part of the Edinburgh Film Festival.

A talk by Bernardo Bertolucci about the movies he had made and the phrase he used stuck in John's mind, "in the cinema we dream with our eyes open." In the bath he dreamt with his eyes shut, but still awake, to avoid drowning.

He felt that dreaming with his eyes open was a perfect way to sum up his favourite pastime, going to the cinema, and he was aware of how the lack of a decent cinema on Kalymnos always bothered him, but he could still enter his dream world in the bath. Entering the cinema on Kalymnos would have to wait.

He enjoyed the cinema at many levels, from intense and thoughtful documentaries to light-hearted romantic comedies and blockbusters.

Never ashamed to admit his taste was anything other than highbrow, he failed to understand why few people attending opening films at the Edinburgh International Film Festival were ever prepared to say at the opening party that they had actually enjoyed the film. Admittedly some of the opening films were not destined to be box office smashes, but with a bit of effort, there was usually some redeeming feature. Possibly the 'cinematerati' would not then appear as cool as they wanted to be thought of, he concluded.

He smiled as he thought back to the screening of a Bjork movie during the Film Festival some years before, when in the movie Bjork was locked into a prison cell and slammed the cover closed on the door's viewing slot. At that point, the entire screen went black. After a few minutes of silence and a black screen, he heard a self-proclaimed expert say, "very Bjork, leaving the audience not knowing what was happening for five minutes." It was not quite so "Bjork" when the bottled water and free Mackie's ice cream were being handed out, along with the apologies about the power cut. At the end of the movie many agreed that the Mackie's ice cream had in fact been the highlight of the entire evening.

John's interest in the cinema started from childhood, when his Uncle Harry took him to see Gulliver's Travels at the Cameo Cinema in Edinburgh, where Harry worked as the projectionist. He remembered clearly climbing up the spiral stairs to the small room with the large rotating reels of film. Looking out of the little window where the beam of light carried the film from the small dark room out onto the large bright screen. Just like in Cinema Paradiso. In the years following, his dad took him to see the Gun Fight at the OK Corral, his first Western. His dad never enjoyed the cinema much, and their next and last visit together was when John, David and Stephen were ejected from the house to allow Elsa to host a Tupperware party. A new concept at the time, which allowed young mums to have a girly night in with a glass of Blue Nun wine and to buy indestructible plastic kitchen containers, many of which survived for decades and were likely to be the downfall of the company. The plastic salad spin-dryer still survived to this day back home in Scotland. This was a centrifuge for lettuce leaves inside a plastic jug which drained every inch of moisture from a washed iceberg or any salad product. How anyone could survive without one was one of life's great mysteries.

Being invited to join the board of the Edinburgh International Film Festival (EIFF) was one of the unexpected perks of being elected to the City Council. The Festival Board was delighted to have someone who actually knew what he was talking about and who had a real interest in film and not someone, as they said, whose main interest was drains.

After his election to Parliament, he was invited to join the London-based EIFF Advisory Board and his involvement with the Film Festival continued after he stepped down from Parliament. This was not an onerous task and involved attending meetings with industry insiders in London and flying the Film Festival flag when possible.

John also joined the All-Party Film Group at Westminster, which often headed off from Westminster on a Wednesday evening, when business finished at 7 pm, to see a recently released movie. The low point of this group was a documentary on a city in China which made millions of socks. That experience alone made every subsequent opening EIFF film a real pleasure.

It was at Film Festival events that John enjoyed meeting celebrities, which was a real contrast to Westminster and always something that went down well later in life, when as an MP he was giving talks to schools or groups in his constituency. Pupils often asked if he had met any famous people, but they were not all that interested in the fact that he had met the Prime Minister or other politicians. They were, however, extremely interested to hear about his meeting with Kylie Minogue at a party at Hopetoun House, a stately home near South Queensferry a few miles outside Edinburgh, or of his meeting with two James Bonds, Sean Connery, and Pierce Brosnan, after film premieres. Also hearing all about the onerous task of looking after Kate Winslet at the opening of her film, Enigma. He was able to say he had met three queens: Queen Elizabeth II at Buckingham Palace and at Holyrood Palace in Edinburgh. the Queen of Pop, Kylie Minogue and the Queen of Country, Dolly Parton, at the Savoy Hotel in London.

However, only Dolly had given him a signed photo, one of Dolly and John together, inscribed with the words, "To John, Love Dolly." He and Carol had also both been invited to Buckingham Palace and to stay over at Holyrood Palace in Edinburgh. These were memories worth passing on to his grandchildren. Even if they were about people they would think were from the far-off and distant past.

Soaking in the bath, John's thoughts floated back to his first Christmas as a Member of Parliament.

He took on the task of organising the new intake Christmas dinner, booking a private dining room in the House of Commons, and inviting the ten newly-elected Liberal Democrat MPs along to their first meal together. It was before most of the new MPs had started to take themselves too seriously and all bar one joined in the fun. Mike Armstrong was the one missing. So, John added a life-size photo of his face to a TV monitor in the corner of the dining room, as if he had joined in by satellite link.

The one honorary member of the 2001 intake was Kath Clarke, MP for Rutland, who had been elected in a by-election the year before and did not have any other intake to join in with. Kath was good company and often happy to join in social activities with the slightest excuse, especially if wine was involved.

The food was going down well, and bottles of wine were being consumed at a steady pace. The secret Santa idea had got everyone into the Christmas mood and in future years some would bring along the same presents from their constituencies year after year. Jack Walker from Orkney and Shetland must have had a stock of Jo Grimond biographies to get rid of and Geoff Cameron, from North Norfolk, clearly believed that promoting a local business was the way forward, as every year, from then on, he brought a tin of Coleman's mustard as his gift. It may have been a secret Santa, but some gifts left a clear trail of origin behind them.

Before the evening ended it was time to introduce The Oscars.

John had bought three copy golden Oscar awards and decided that the categories for nominations were to be 'Moustache of the Year,' 'The One to Watch' and an excuse was found to award an Oscar to Patsy Calton, the new MP for Cheadle, as Patsy had just been given the all clear, ten years after suffering from breast cancer. Little could they know that by the time of the next election Patsy's cancer would return with a vengeance and that John and her good friend Claire Burdett would wheel her into the chamber just after their re-election, as by that time she was unable to walk. For the first and last time, the Speaker came down from his seat to welcome her home. She died only weeks later.

Assuming he was the sole nominee for 'Moustache of the Year,' David McDonald, and his luxuriant moustache, was about to make his acceptance speech, when he noticed that the usually clean-shaven Walker and Cameron were suddenly sporting a Mexican long black mouser and a silver/grey 'tash to match Geoff's silver hair.

McDonald was a true gentleman and as ever dealt with this threat to his award with the panache few in the room could hope to match. He was once described as the only MP who believed the

Barnett Formula was something he should put on his hair. The double of Lord Lucan, missing for many years after his murdered nanny was discovered, McDonald had left the Lords and stood for election to the Commons. A remarkable feat, never to be repeated.

Before John had announced the competition, he supplied both interlopers with stick-on moustaches bought at a joke shop in Edinburgh along with the Oscar statues. The Oscar statuette being awarded also had a small black moustache stuck onto it and before David McDonald could make his acceptance speech, Jack had removed a small part of his black moustache and stuck it onto the face on the TV monitor. The small black moustache below his nose, the staring look and the hair combed smoothly to one side over part of his forehead in an all too familiar style left Mike Armstrong clearly looking too scary for it to pass without comment. All to be caught on camera by John, who kept the photos but then banned cameras from all future dinners, with everyone's agreement.

The 'One to Watch' category was decided by secret ballot and was won by Jack Walker. He was reminded that it could mean he was a potential rising star, or a dodgy character and that we needed to keep an eye on him. That would be left to history to decide.

After the secret ballot, Andy Brown, the new MP for York, mentioned to Jack that he was surprised to have received so few votes. He later confided to John that he believed he was the only one of the new intake who could become a future leader of the party, as he 'modestly' explained to John, in the Commons Tea Room, that the new leader would not only need to be young, he would need to be good looking too and that Andy was the only one who fitted both categories. John did not add that the new leader would also need to be an MP and hold on to his seat.

As Andy was the only one of the newly elected MPs not to be re-elected at the next election, his leadership ambitions ended more quickly than he had planned.

When the dinner came to an end most of the new intake drifted towards the unlocked Commons debating chamber, Richard Jones confronted John aggressively, in Lib-Dem terms, with a wagging finger and shouting with a slurred voice, demanding to know why he had not been called to speak much at the dinner.

As the dinner wore on, to keep order, the formalities of the debating chamber had ended up in the dining room, with John in the role of Speaker and others being called by him to speak, while interventions and points of order were taken. Cleary, Ricky had felt snubbed and was pissed, in more ways than one. It looked like he might take a swing at John, when Jack joined in, and pulled him back, shouting "Ricky, he's not worth it," with a fine Bianca from Eastenders accent. If ever there was any doubt that laughter is the best medicine to relieve tension, here it was.

They wandered into the main chamber, many the worse for wear, and John stood at the opposition despatch box, feeling what it would be like to be on the front bench, or even leader of the opposition, while Jack stood at the government's dispatch box to begin the debate. Not to be outdone Oliver Brown positioned himself comfortably in the Speaker's chair, while those colleagues still standing took seats on the green benches in the chamber. The debate went on with interventions and points of order, until the "Speaker" fell asleep.

No member of the security staff in Parliament has ever been sacked. Many put this down to the fact that they have access to the security camera tapes which cover every inch of the building, twenty-four hours a day and seven days a week.

New intake Christmas Dinners in future years developed into slightly more sober affairs, with one exception: when Paul Marsden defected from the Labour Party and joined the Lib-Dems.

After much debate, he was invited to join the now famous 2001 intake Christmas Dinner, but thankfully he did not appear. Instead, John included an Oscar for best poem in the award categories, as Paul had become notorious for his sexually explicit poems he had unwisely put online. This was John's first Oscar triumph, with an ode to Paul. In that same year Oliver Brown, who had never won an Oscar, quietly approached John to see if this situation could be remedied. Happy to oblige, a new category of 'Man Least Likely to Win an Oscar' was devised and all three nominees were Oliver.

As he was about to receive his Oscar, the decision to award him was challenged by ex-lawyer Jack Walker, who deemed that he could not be awarded the Oscar, as the award would make him ineligible for the category. To this day Oliver Brown has no Oscar.

Another highlight, or low point, of the new intake Christmas Dinner, was when John organised the Party Leader, Charles Kennedy, to make a guest appearance and award an Oscar. Word of the 2001 Christmas Dinner had spread to all other Lib-Dem MPs, including the leader and he was honoured to have been asked. The only guest, or outsider, ever invited to attend the dinners was Shirley Williams, and while she was great company, she was also teetotal and others felt constrained by her sobriety. The wine consumption at that dinner was at an all-time low. John banned guests from all future 2001 intake Christmas Dinners.

Shirley must have had a soft spot for John as she told him some years later that when she heard he was stepping down from Parliament it broke her heart. She also inscribed his copy of her book, *Climbing the Bookshelves*, with the same message.

In the run-up to the 2005 Christmas Dinner, at which Charles had agreed to make the Oscar presentation, nobody could have foreseen the turmoil about to unfold in the party that evening, as a leadership crisis consumed the party and was summed up in an Evening Standard billboard, "Lib-Dem Leader Charles Kennedy – Doomed."

It would take more than a crisis in the party to cancel the dinner, even on the day half of the Parliamentary Party withdrew their support for Charles, which set in motion the events which would eventually result in his resignation as party leader. On that same day, he presented an Oscar at the Christmas dinner, supported by his deputy, Simon, who appeared with him, ready to take over, if he should ever be called upon to do so.

Following a few more long soaks in the bath and memories of the past, it became all too clear to John what he must now do, in the immediate future.

Chapter 6
It's The Economy, Stupid

The first view of Kalymnos visitors see is the harbour, the main street, a row of shops and restaurants and the Mayor's office, the most imposing building overlooking the seafront. Every visitor arrives by ferry, mostly from Kos and a much smaller number from other islands. Many were not with tour companies and needed two things immediately, a place to eat and somewhere to stay.

The problem was that the ferries were now arriving more than half empty. John knew that while the overall number of tourists had dropped significantly, there were still more than enough arriving at Kos airport to give Kalymnos a real boost, if he could just get to them first and convince them Kalymnos was worth visiting. Many came from the UK and most of the others spoke English, the Scandinavians better than most. Communication with them should not be a problem. There were other problems he would have to address, if things were to change.

The issue of the timing of the last regular ferry crossing and how to attract customers from the regular late flights needed to be sorted out and neither was insurmountable.

As well as the normal ferry, whose last sailing left Kos at 7 pm, there were operators who would provide a boat to take small groups of passengers on scenic sails, sunset tours, and day trips to neighbouring islands such as Leros and Pserimos. They had comfortable boats, were safe, and they would welcome the opportunity to pick up more business. The extra ferry trips could also provide access to more potential customers for their regular tours.

John checked out the best operator and found someone who was happy to work with him and to be flexible. He designed and printed improved literature, advertising their regular tours and offered the boat owner exclusive access to everyone he brought over from Kos, in return for the captain guaranteeing to leave Mastahari forty-five minutes after the flight landed at Kos airport, even for delayed flights. A fixed ferry fare was agreed and the first link in the chain was ready.

Taxis, which normally sat in what was known locally as 'taxi square' in Pothia waiting for fares were told that they could get guaranteed fares if they were at the harbour at specific times. Fixed fares were set again to different parts of the island and publicised on a clear sign. The habit of fleecing customers needed to be broken. The taxi drivers had to learn that regular reasonable fares, and good tips from satisfied customers provided more income than one large, overpriced fare, which would put off customers from using taxis for the rest of their stay.

A bus at Kos airport was the next issue to be resolved, as was good quality accommodation on the island - at the right price.

On the island of Kos there were two ports where ferries would leave for Kalymnos, the main town of Kos, or the smaller harbour with a shorter crossing to Kalymnos, from Mastahari. Normally the regular bus would go from the airport to Kos town and much later would arrive at Mastahari. Tourists arriving for the first time had no idea what route the bus should take and after some negotiation, the bus driver was happy to accept twenty euros for each journey, for making a minor change to his route taking his bus to Kos, via Mastahari. This would provide an instant reliable method of getting tourists quickly from the airport to the harbour where the ferry was waiting. The next task was to have good clean reasonable accommodation ready on Kalymnos.

John had stopped over at enough places on the island to know which locations were good for families with children, others which had better nightlife or restaurants close by and more remote locations for those who wanted a quiet time. There were many willing hotel owners in all areas delighted at the prospect of business improving and everyone welcomed his proposals to bring more business to the island. There was still a suspicion that they could not work out what he was getting out of it for himself - as nobody did anything for nothing, or so they thought.

Restaurant owners soon heard about the plan to get more business on the island and a few asked John how to make sure their menus were appealing to as many people as possible. Following Gordon Ramsay's basic guide of reducing the number of choices on the menu but making sure the dishes were good value, made from fresh local ingredients and authentic dishes, rather than chips with everything, was the answer. The restaurant owners soon found the locals noticed the improvement and liked it too.

Tour companies in the past had driven such a hard bargain that accommodation owners in places like Katina Studios near Myrties had signed up to give over every bedroom for the entire season for as little as twenty euros per night. Desperate times followed the withdrawal of the tour companies and prices had sunk so low that the only way the owners could keep them at that level was to offer little or no service.

Rooms were not as clean as they should be, air conditioning was not as reliable as it needed to be in the Greek summer heat, swimming pools were not well serviced, with neither fresh towels nor poolside drinks and the general standard of service had slipped below what most visitors now expected. If this did not change, those who were convinced to visit once would never return.

At the risk of alienating some hotels and other restaurants who were stuck in a rut and did not want to change, John worked with those who were happy to follow his lead, improve what they needed to, and then deliver a level of service they had previously no conception of.

John had stayed in hostels, cheap hotels, and the best of hotels over many years and while he was no expert, he was acutely aware of what people wanted and what needed to change.

Bedrooms needed to be not only clean, but they also needed to smell fresh, all linen had to be spotless and changed regularly. Towels with the texture of sandpaper needed to be replaced and air conditioning needed to work all the time, not only after a complaint, a long delay and the repair man being called.

Breakfast needed to give visitors a good start to the day. Fresh fruit, Greek yoghurt, honey, good quality tea and coffee, cereals, fresh milk, and a variety of fresh locally baked bread would easily do the trick, and all other meals could be eaten out. Most of all, the hosts had to make the guests have a great time and make sure they would come back and bring their friends next time.

Everything was now in place, and it was time to put the plan into action.

The first flight to Kos airport targeted by John and his three enthusiastic young paid helpers arrived late, as expected, and while the exhausted tourists waited in the heat of the overcrowded airport for their bags, they were given the full treatment. They were first offered free bottles of cold water, while they were politely offered cheap transport to Mastahari, a calm cool ferry crossing to Kalymnos with the prospect of seeing dolphins in the sea leading the boat towards its destination.

A leaflet detailing the attractions of Kalymnos was left with each passenger, giving them time to consider their options. The literature contained a few comparisons to the overcrowded, overdeveloped Kos, as well as a choice of accommodation suitable for everyone. People were given a quick clear choice, not hurried, but left aware that there was one good destination and one not quite so good. The prices were competitive, low enough to be attractive but high enough to give the hotel owners the best deal they had received in a long time. Those on package holidays were ignored, as they headed for their pre-arranged tour buses, but there were plenty of others to aim for. Independent travellers, backpackers, and island hoppers, but too few families, as most with children had not risked coming without planning their accommodation in advance.

John made a mental note to contact an old colleague, Bruce Simpson, before the end of the day, to set up a website with details of the accommodation John was dealing with, to have it online as soon as possible.

Before he realised it, he had more than enough people to declare the first day's operation a success. The transport to Mastahari worked a treat and the ferry was there ready and waiting for them. John's helpers gave a hand with the bags and waved the ferry off. His student workforce on Kos not only had the positive attitude to keep the flagging tourists in good spirits, they would also be his eyes and ears, to keep him informed of any reaction on Kos. The ferry left as soon as the last person was on board.

One unexpected surprise was to meet a group who had regularly used this route and had usually slept on the beach sunbeds overnight or had paid for an overpriced room at the one rundown hotel at Mastahari harbour. This was the service they had been waiting for and they were willing and ready to join in with the new 'high speed' link.

As if by design, a pod of dolphins appeared to lead the boat across the straits towards the harbour at Pothia. The sun was setting, the town looked inviting, and the evening was cooling down as the ferry reached the port. Standing to attention was a row of taxi drivers ready and willing to make friends with their new customers.

On the forty-minute sail each new visitor had time to decide where they would be staying for at least their first night and before landing a quick phone call let every hotel owner know exactly how many guests would be arriving.

Welcome groups would be in place for everyone at each hotel or taverna reception and all guests were now guaranteed the perfect start to their first Kalymnion experience.

The impact on the island was immediate. Everyone wanted in on the new system. Eventually, John identified people capable of running everything without him being so hands-on. Maintaining the quality of the service was the key.

The website was now up and running and Bruce had developed a mini booking.com type of website for those hotels working with John, but they had already become aware of those resisting his plans and John had worked out how to deal with them.

His Kos workers had picked up and passed on details of those who would soon be taking action to spike the foreigner's guns.

Chapter 7
The Resistance

It was not long before word of the increased numbers of people leaving Kos for a holiday on Kalymnos reached the ears of those who could cause problems for John, and the entire operation.

Many Greeks enjoyed a feeling of self-importance and were quick to share their thoughts, with those who would listen, about what they were planning to do. Fortunately for John, he had a line into the pubs and coffee shops in Kos town where his helpers worked. They were John's best source of local information. Knowing what the opposition might be planning was one campaign weapon he was always happy to keep in his armoury.

Early on in his thinking, he had calculated that this was going to happen, and he developed two alternative strategies for dealing with the problem. One was going to be hard and the other, soft. The hard option was to take on people head-on and not budge an inch. He knew that those who thought he could be pushed around easily would try to do so and he was having none of it. If they met strong resistance, many Greeks would bluster angrily but lacked the determination and would avoid the work required to follow up talk with action. The softer strategy was to offer a level

of help to those willing to follow his lead and to
benefit those on Kos, by learning from what was
happening on Kalymnos.

One other advantage of this two-pronged
approach was to split any opposition into
two factions and leave them arguing amongst
themselves much of the time, before and if ever
they could agree on how to proceed. No group
of Greek men could agree on anything quickly
and highly animated discussions, or what looked
like arguments to foreigners, would be observed
in cafes, when all that was actually going on was
nothing more than a discussion about how much
sugar was required in a coffee.

He was aware that the tourist season did not last
long, and time was of the essence. The success of
the first season needed to be established quickly,
so that he could get going with his many other
ideas, before booking for the next year's season
started.

Bruce now had the website up and running and
all teething problems were sorted. He was already
receiving enquiries about accommodation for next
year, from those who had experienced a great
time this season and he was pressing John for
information about room rates and availability. His
statistical analysis also showed that those happy
on their first visit were planning to bring more

people next time. His site had been getting good reviews in the travel media and the TripAdvisor reviews he was reading were the icing on the cake. Online business was growing steadily.

John had given thought to every link in the chain and had used his previous approach of placing himself in the opposition's shoes to see where they might make problems for him. There were many potential weak links to be strengthened. Access to the harbour at Mastahari, the use of the bus and its diverted route was a real weakness and the ferry was less of a problem as the owner was self-employed and answered to nobody, and marketing in the airport might be an issue, but the airport was usually so chaotic that there was little he could see developing into a problem. He concluded that the new route the bus was taking was something that now needed some more thought.

It was too good to last. At first, he thought that the airport taxi drivers might prove to be a problem, but their destination of choice was not Mastahari, but Kos town, as it was a better fare on a longer route and took them to where their next hire would most likely be.

If the diverted bus route could not continue for any reason, the answer was to provide his own service, hire a bus and get the hotels who ended up with paying guests to work together to pay for it initially, until it generated enough income to pay for itself. It did not take long to find that one hotel owner on Kalymnos had a cousin on Kos with a bus and the day the driver of the regular route announced, as expected, that his boss had stopped him from using his new route to the ferry and receiving his 20-euro daily bonus, was the day the new service started.

The harbourmaster at Mastahari had clearly been pressurised, or bribed, to make life difficult for the new ferry service to Kalymnos and he was all too smug as he sat back and watched the problems of access to the ferry increase, as visitors struggled in the heat to drag cases along the long walk from the bus to the ferry past his 'road closed' sign and other obstacles strategically left in their way.

Time for direct action, John thought, as he announced angrily to the harbourmaster a total boycott of the harbour by all traffic from Kalymnos. He knew he had no authority to do this and that most of those on Kalymnos would not agree to any boycott at all, as the harbour charges in the larger Kos harbour were twice those at Mastahari. John knew that it was not about the truth, it was all about confidence, not looking as if it was an issue that bothered him, and that he would happily divert his ferry to Kos town with all other business following. The harbourmaster's broken English was his problem and John's improved Greek was now an advantage, as he walked away predicting the harbour would be dead from lack of traffic by the end of the week. The perspiration was running down from his forehead as he walked away, glad that his nervousness was not as visible as he could feel it in the pit of his stomach.

In total panic, the harbourmaster cracked and pleaded with John not to call a boycott of his harbour, he had a family depending on the harbour and they would lynch him if their incomes stopped. Problem number two - solved.

Problem number three was the Mayor of Kos and his cousin, who was the Mayor of Kalymnos. They were used to having things their own way, without the interference of outsiders. They did not see the need for change, especially if they were not getting the credit for it, or at least an income from it.

Kos was too much of a problem and there were too many issues for John to get involved in or side-tracked with on the larger island. He met with the Mayor, and wore his only suit and tie, which also confirmed that he was a man of importance. He returned to MP mode; over a glass of iced tea, he mentioned a few of the important Greeks he had met in London including the Ambassador and Minister for Tourism. He pulled a rabbit out of the

hat when he mentioned that he was one of the
MPs who had raised the issue and had laid down
an Early Day Motion in Parliament for the return
of the Elgin Marbles to Athens, and with his party
now in Government he could pick up the phone
to friends and former colleagues who were now
Government Ministers.

He did not reveal that he had already spoken to
his old colleague Vince Cable, the new Business
Minister in the UK but about another issue. The
Mayor was used to local politics, but he knew this
was out of his league and this was well above his
pay grade.

John then got down to the nitty-gritty and
knowing that, to a large degree, all politics is local,
he moved away from national issues and on to
local politics. He spelt out a few ideas he could
use to improve life on Kos, the Mayor's island, and
with the local elections coming up in a year's time
the Mayor was keen to do everything possible to
ensure his re-election.

In return for John's help and advice on a few local
issues and not wishing to risk being the reason
the British Government might not return the Elgin
Marbles, he agreed to back off from causing any
more problems. What happened on Kalymnos was
not really of much concern to him. He could not
however speak for his cousin Nikolas, who was

altogether more hot-headed and on Kalymnos, he was already badmouthing John whenever he could. Not completely taken in by the Mayor's offer of neutrality, John made sure spare tyres were kept ready for when his new bus service had their tyres slashed – and they were.

Two things were now happening at the same time. The opposition from Nikolas was becoming a pain in the neck and he was using his influence, friends, employees and more to make life difficult for John and those who appreciated John's contribution to the island. Others were enjoying his company and exploring new ways of improving the island. His understanding of the language was much improved, but he decided only to speak English. He had found that his best method of finding out what was actually going on was to have a blank look on his face when the locals spoke Greek.

The locals enjoyed learning, or improving, their English and while most youngsters on the island were now taught it at school, their parents were lagging behind them and it was now an essential tool they needed to use, as it was the language spoken by the majority of visitors to the island.

Most people were happy to listen to John and his fountain of ideas kept flowing. Locals enjoyed translating his English into what they thought he was talking about and putting their own interpretation on it, as if it had been their idea in the first place.

Improved recycling and better rubbish collection would cut down their costs and with no alternative other than burning the rest of the waste this was a serious issue. Islanders had long complained about the toxic plume which blew their way when the wind changed direction. Exploring EU funding for wind generation and solar power would save money and reduce their reliance on the ageing power station.

Passing a local by-law to ensure all who used motorbikes and scooters wore crash helmets would save lives and reduce the worry many parents had about their children being injured. Hardly a day passed without an accident and the island hospital was far from able to cope with anything other than minor injuries. Sadly, some teenagers were left with broken bones, and a few had been left paralysed or brain-damaged following fairly minor crashes or accidents.

One person was taking in the new optimistic mood on the island, and looking out from the Mayor's office, under the large terra cotta domes of the town hall overlooking the harbour, he surveyed what he considered 'his' island. He had had enough of John and his fan club, as he called it.

The Mayor was a short balding man, who often wore a suit that was too tight over a shirt that needed both washed and ironed. The fact that he sweated a lot and did not shower enough was never raised with him, as nobody dared to do anything other than compliment him and no one would ever contradict him. Never a man to see any issue with his appearance, like many men on the island, he considered himself not only extremely good-looking but also a real catch for any woman whose bottom he patted in an all too creepy manner.

Nikolas was about to put a spike the guns of those who were no longer entirely dependent on him for favours. He could see exactly how he was being side-lined by this foreigner and he was not about to sit back and let that happen. Everyone knew everyone on the island, and many were related to dozens of others. Nikolas had drawn up a list of those he would make life difficult for and was calculating how he could pull them back into line.

One he did not want back into line was *the tourist*, he refused to use John's name and *'tourist'* was often used as a disparaging term to describe those who had no real interest on the island, had lower moral standards and would take what they wanted, then leave. He wanted *the tourist* to vanish as soon as possible, and he was confident that by the end of the summer he would be gone for good, along with his friends.

John was at the top of his hit list, as he soon found out, when his electricity supply was cut off. Others had problems with their water supply, rubbish was left uncollected from shop owners who had appeared too friendly to the tourist and worse of all was the abuse of power when the children of John's new friends began to have a tough time at school. Teachers were not immune to the influence of Nikolas. In his mind, John thought of him as Nasty Nick, one of the bad guys on the TV show Big Brother many years ago. A real shit, if there ever was one.

One by one, the locals began to distance themselves from John, as they were either entirely in the control of the Mayor and his influence, or dependent on council services. Complaints about power supplies only resulted in records of their paid bills going missing, rubbish left uncollected soon began to smell in the heat of the Greek summer and often rats would then appear.

Most new houses on the island had been built with large water storage tanks in the basements and could cope with a break in the mains water supply, but many older residents had no such tanks in their homes and they could not cope with carrying heavy jerry cans of water from the taps in the village. It was too much for many of them and slowly John found that he was finding more spare time on his hands as people found excuses to give him a swerve. He began to spend more time reading, writing, and playing his guitar.

Still, the ideas about how to improve the island kept coming and with the help of a local printer, he decided to share his ideas in a small free newsletter delivered to every home on Kalymnos, including the most remote houses on the island.

Printing costs had reduced in recent years, and he knew roughly how long it would take to deliver to every home. For many people designing, printing, and delivering ten thousand leaflets is a daunting task. For John, it was nothing compared to the fifty thousand leaflets per week a full-blown election campaign would go through. This was a small-scale operation for him, and he had missed campaigning since standing down. This was just his cup of tea.

Back in Edinburgh, he could easily deliver 150 leaflets per hour. The island's population was around twenty thousand, so the ten thousand houses would still take some time, even if he only managed one hundred every hour. He factored in lots of stops to chat, a long break in the middle of the day, when it was really hot and not knowing many areas, he would no doubt get lost even in small villages.

Delivering to each house he got to know the island, the people, the issues and how people felt about them. It reminded him of how he had started campaigning in the community in his Edinburgh neighbourhood. It was why he entered politics – not to get elected, but to improve things locally.

There were fewer than the ten thousand houses he had estimated, as, unlike in the UK, many generations lived in one home or lived together in a sub-divided home. The tradition of handing over the house to the daughter on her wedding day in practice, for some families, meant handing over the ownership, but still living in the house the daughter and her husband would move into. In later life, the daughter would then care for her elderly parents who had given them a home. It was their much more civilised alternative to elderly people ending up lonely and in care homes.

People got to know him, and he still found delight in discovering hidden homes tucked away in surprising places. In one rural area back home, his friend and election agent Dave Watson discovered a remote caravan with a naked male occupant who enjoyed wandering about outside even in the cold weather. He challenged John to find it, which he did. John used to joke that he was not sure of this man's voting intentions but that on one visit when talking to him, he had noticed a distinct swing to the right.

Before he knew it, local people who enjoyed his newsletter, half in English and half in Greek, were looking forward to the next issue and some were now volunteering to help him deliver it. Many felt sorry for the hot and sweating foreigner who always looked exhausted. John looked tired, but with his regular exercise, he had already noticed an improvement in his stamina and the loss of a few pounds. The newsletter was free and informative, and it gave people something to chat about, which families loved, as many were much more family orientated than community-minded. Many were also obsessed with what was going on in every family member's life, but now there were other issues being discussed. It reminded him of his old *Focus* newsletters, so he called it *Focus on Kalymnos*. He enjoyed photography and took his camera with him when he was out and about. With digital technology, photos taken one day could be printed in the *Focus* and delivered, all within the week.

As the interest in the newsletter grew, and the number of volunteers delivering also increased, he had to increase the size from A4 to A3 folded in two. Four pages of text forced him to keep it short and interesting. This size was easy and cheap to print and coped with the increasing content, which now included a couple of adverts for local businesses and details of wider public interest, like local events and concerts. The news sheet became a fortnightly production, and it was now being delivered within 48 hours of its return from the printers. Those delivering it felt a sense of pride that they were the ones local residents would pass on issues to and they enjoyed pre-publication discussions about the content. They also collected feedback forms, which were included on the back page of every *Focus* asking people to jot down a note on anything they wanted to say or issues they were concerned with.

The lack of safe play areas for the younger children was raised again and again. The parks, or smaller play areas, were a disaster and with nothing for children to do in them. Dangerous surfaces and worst of all, broken glass and discarded syringes had been found more than once, giving every mother their worst nightmare that their child might be infected with something from one of the small, but increasing, number of drug users on the island. Playgrounds were generally left to those who wanted somewhere to gather after dark, where nobody would see them.

One other issue John highlighted in *Focus* was that of the busy main road around the harbour, which was the main route for cars, buses, trucks and the many noisy motor-scooters and motorbikes on the island and the danger this road caused to anyone not in a car or lorry. Just behind the street of harbour-front shops and restaurants was an unused maze of small winding lanes and streets of empty shops and run-down or old abandoned houses, now only used as stores and parking spaces. Only motorbikes and scooters used them as they were too narrow for cars and vans, and many pedestrians, especially the elderly and children, avoided the risks of the motorbikes and just had to take their chances beside the busy harbour road.

John knew many of the owners of the derelict properties and suggested that the owners of the properties in the small streets get together and push for the small narrow lanes to become pedestrian-only zones. This was a new concept, as motor vehicles ruled, and for years people were used to risking life and limb every time they went out. The thought of a pedestrian zone had supporters, but most believed it would not work as nobody would obey the rules.

The houses and disused shops and stores in the lanes, with a little work, could make perfect cheaper, or backpacker-type accommodation, especially for the new breed of cost-conscious young independent travellers who were now appearing in greater numbers. The small shops below them could be advertised to artists and craftsmen, who would not compete with the owners' existing shops on the main road, but who would open up for the tourist season. This would provide a welcome boost to their income in the tough times being experienced by everyone. Many small businesses employed a few family members and most also had fit young men with the strength and spare time to do much of the building work required.

John knew he could get Bruce to provide a website offering to advertise the accommodation and shops if they ever materialised, and it could attract a new wave of artists and crafters to the island. He even planned to take one himself and stock it with Carol's paintings and sculptures from Archipelago, which he had previously sold when he and Carol ran a pop-up gallery in one of his shops in Edinburgh.

Some of the best photographs John had taken were in the lanes. The mix of colours on old walls, doors and window shutters, the detail of the buildings and the style of the old buildings and balconies with cats appearing from every window with some finding shade from the bright sunlight, all made very appealing images, and the draft website link emailed to John was perfect. Although it had not yet gone live, John could show Bruce's ideas to the property owners and they were stunned by the photo-shopped images he had produced, as he had removed the many ugly

garbage bins, cables and wires and other unsightly aspects of the area, then inserted a few creative improvements, such as good walking surfaces and café awnings, to make the revived area the most attractive area on the island.

Focus developed into a vehicle for those interested in the community and as the editor, John would be invited to events in the hope that he would include a flattering photo of the organisers, or a positive comment about what had been happening. There was nothing the locals enjoyed more than reading about themselves, or knowing their neighbours and friends were reading good things about them.

The issue of improving the town centre was building up a head of steam and a public meeting was called by the shop owners. John was asked to chair it, along with an interpreter. On the night of the meeting - all hell broke loose.

Those who were for change were faced by a bunch of thugs who arrived along with the Mayor, who put a spoke into every positive idea mentioned by anyone. The evening went from bad to worse when the subject moved away from the topic under discussion to personal insults and name-calling. The tension was, as ever, fuelled by alcohol and it was not long before the first punch was swung. It was like the wild west.

Never one to be involved in a fight, John remembered one night outside the Caledonian Hotel in Edinburgh, where he and another passer-by tried to pull an attacker off a man lying on the pavement, who was being kicked by his assailant. The attacker swung round and head-butted the other good Samaritan in the face. His nose appeared to explode, and blood was everywhere. Since then, John had always used his quick turn of speed to remove himself from anywhere trouble was brewing. This time there was no escape.

John called for calm, but nobody was listening, and he ended the meeting. It was too late to stop what had been started, and as the first chair flew through the window onto the street it attracted more people from outside to enter the hall and join in the "fun."

The scene of devastation looked like an earthquake had struck. John assumed that the entire project for improving the town had come to an end, but it was not to be.

In the cold light of day, after the wounds had healed, the locals continued to talk about the details of the changes he had suggested, and Bruce's images had caught their imagination. Some started to notice, for the first time, the potential in the property they owned.

Many had also enjoyed the rumble, as there had not been a good fight for years, and most of the women who patched up their wounds enjoyed seeing their men on the receiving end for a change. Some Greek men still considered that a good slap did their wives the "world of good." Many women also believed the Mayor was a complete shit, whose number would soon be up, as the four yearly Mayoral election was fast approaching and that his lack of concern for the future of the island, especially for the women and children on it, would come back and bite him where it hurt most – in his wallet.

The older women on the island spoke to each other about every issue, from the local problems to the international concerns of the day, when the men were out of the way, but did not share their opinions with their husbands, brothers, or even male friends.

It was a society where the men ruled the roost or believed they did. The men on Kalymnos were notorious for having affairs, or other women kept by them, and when their wives complained, older women often recommended to young women that having another baby would answer their problems and keep them busy. John heard one older woman telling a young newlywed woman, "When you get married, you are signing up for a life of misery."

The 21st century and equality still had a long way to go on mainland Greece and even more so on most small islands. The women were also discussing many of the issues raised in *Focus on Kalymnos*.

Being just off the main road, the older properties in the lanes had not suffered from any modernisation and there were some stylish and classic buildings of high quality and others with intricate wrought iron balconies and handrails and fine detailed original plasterwork. A few posts and chains and bollards could easily stop the bikers and before long the lanes could then come back to life, a few of the more thoughtful owners reckoned.

The older residents remembered how the lanes used to be, just after the war and into the 1950s. They were safe, with no traffic, cool and stylish and the younger islanders could hopefully start to enjoy the traditional side of the island, by opening small cafes for both younger and older people, away from the tourist hordes, and in winter, when some of the larger seasonal places closed new small-scale businesses could develop. A few places with live traditional music could then open later in the evening as used to be the way. The grandparents were the most enthusiastic of all about the proposed changes.

Chapter 8
Surprise Visitors

Out of the blue, he heard voices he instantly recognised, "Papa, hi dad, Johnny" it was Sarah, George, and the kids. They came at least once every year for a holiday and to visit their extended Greek family. What a perfect way to start the day. They had kept the timing of their visit a surprise and it would be great to have the large house bursting with activity again. The house, their home, had been too quiet, for too long.

He hugged the children, who spoke fluent Greek, but always spoke to him in English. They were as happy as any children could be at the start of their summer holidays, but his ears detected a tension between Sarah and George and neither of them was aware that he could now follow most of their Greek discussion. In Edinburgh, they often spoke in Greek and now it was becoming clear that it was not just to suit George, who was always happier to speak his native tongue, it was to cover some of the issues they did not want John to know anything about.

John had not had too much to do with George's family on the island, as there were so many of them. While John had no parents or grandparents alive and just two cousins, both living in Australia,

George has 56 cousins and approximately 400 living relatives, mostly living on Kalymnos. The only way for John to enjoy life and relative peace on the island was to avoid the family get-togethers, eating and drinking and his supposed inability to speak Greek allowed him to stay away from the family - without causing too much offence. This would now end, and the first family 'invasion' would be within 24 hours, he predicted. He was right.

George's sister, Hope, arrived with her children and husband, Nick, a lovely quiet man, a carpenter and a good bouzouki player. He was always happy and looked content while saying little. Parents and the grandmother soon appeared, each bringing food; tzatziki, stuffed olives, bread, skewers with chicken, pork, and vegetables and more and more. As the evening wore on the chat increased and John maintained his pretend lack of understanding of all but the most basic Greek phrases. He had a phrase book and when he mastered useless sayings such as, "can you fix my central heating" a great cheer would go up. No reply from the Greek family was ever understood by him, or so everyone thought.

It soon became evident that all was not well in Sarah and George's relationship, and still, he decided to say nothing, play with the children, enjoy their company, and let them get on with whatever the problem was. John had tried to advise different family members in the past and found that usually it ended with those family members doing exactly what they wanted to, regardless of his advice, and he became frustrated at the time and energy he would put in just to have it ignored. It was his daughter Sarah, who pointed this out to him, and he had to admit, she was right, and it then saved him hours of wasted time and energy.

Staying quiet was not easy and the loss of a younger brother some years before, to suicide, always left him wondering if he could have said and done any more to help him. His brother had decided to stop taking his medication for manic depression and feeling fine, made what he thought was a rational decision to end it all, as he must have thought his wife and young children would be better off without him.

John would never stop worrying about those he loved, especially Maria, but in the end, he knew that he could not fix everything. He also knew that worrying never actually solved anything or produced a solution to any problem. Pulling back from issues that he could leave to others did not come easily, but he enjoyed the time it freed up for him to work on other more pressing matters that he could actually do something about.

The next two weeks consisted of complete relaxation, playing with the children at the beach and hotel pools, meals out, boat trips and swimming in the sea. He was now experiencing first-hand exactly why the tourists were coming back to the island. He loved it and it reminded him exactly why it was important to make sure he did what he could to help the island avoid the worst of times.

If Sarah and George had 'issues' he would leave it to them to deal with. He had enjoyed the break and as he waved them off at the harbour, the dolphins, as if on cue, appeared to lead their boat back to Mastahari.

In the distance, from his office window, Nasty Nick was watching, hoping that John would have returned with his family. Time to turn up the heat, he thought.

Chapter 9
Park Life

Locals had been taken with the idea in one *Focus* of improving one particularly neglected park and John had gathered together a group of interested parents, mostly local mothers, but also an English couple who had settled on Telendos, the small island separated from Kalymnos by an earthquake over 400 years ago. The couple, Tom and Suzie had started to feel isolated on Telendos and wanted to get involved in a project to help them integrate with the locals. Originally, they thought it might just involve clearing up the play area, but John had much grander ideas.

Some time ago, when he was an MP, a local contractor, ERDC, who employed over 200 people, contacted him to ask if he would visit their headquarters building, which was on an industrial estate near Newbridge, a small village close to Edinburgh Airport. They supplied artificial turf for football pitches and other sports arenas and had an impressive client base. John had been aware of the controversial plastic surfaces which had been tried and rejected by football clubs in England, with all but one exception. He did not expect to be surprised on his visit to their HQ, but he was.

The quality of the new artificial grass was more

like grass than some real grass, he thought, and instead of it feeling like course plastic, the grass had a soft natural feel, enhanced by small rubber granules where the earth would be on a natural surface. The smooth surface had the texture of the real thing. The preparation and laying of the new artificial playing surface had advanced over decades and it was no longer subject to the problems experienced in the early years. The end result was that the new playing surfaces were being installed worldwide and the company, based at Newbridge, was tendering for contracts throughout Europe and Africa.

Their immediate problem was not finding work, as their order book was full, but being paid for work already done and one particular problem they could not resolve was with a London University. After a few phone calls to the Department of Education, a coffee with a Junior Minister and then one meeting with the University, which had been suffering from cash flow problems, they eventually paid up. The CEO had said that if he could ever do anything for John, he should just ask. Now was the time. He was just in time, as the company was about to go into liquidation, hit by late payments and big project delays, the workforce had now been reduced to 79. Fortunately, John's contact was still there, and he was glad to help an old friend before the liquidators moved in.

The steel container arrived in the Pothia harbour side and was craned into the holding area. More deliveries of non-perishable items were being delivered to Kalymnos by container and although it was far from being a container port, it was a convenient way to bring a range of goods and products onto the island.

The park master plan was finally agreed upon, and fundraising was well underway. The main event was to be a concert held at the park to say farewell to the old playpark for one last time before work started. This playground was particularly unpopular with parents as it was effectively a piece of wasteland, the swings had been broken and not repaired, and the ground was strewn with sharp small stones and broken glass. As it was the only football pitch in that part of the island, children often returned home with cuts and grazes, but worst of all it had become a hang-out for unsavoury characters and discarded syringes had been found there by young children.

The village committee had other priorities and were happy to pass the buck, and any costs, on to John and his enthusiastic group to see what, if anything, they could do to improve the playground area.

Fortunately, local parks were not under the jurisdiction of the Mayor's office, or no doubt

he would have done his best to try to stop
this project as well. Parks on the island were a
village responsibility, and the one about to be
transformed was next to *Sugar*, a restaurant close
to the crossroads at Chorio, the old capital of
the island, on the busy road north from Pothia
to Myrties and Massouri. As well as a few shops,
restaurants and cafes, the crossroad also had a bus
stop, where children would meet before and after
school. The location was perfect, thought John,
as it would not only benefit lots of children from
various parts of the island outside Pothia it would
be seen by many more, who could take pride in the
project and might possibly want to do the same
elsewhere. Parks in Pothia town were under the
jurisdiction of Nasty Nick and every single one,
with the exception of the one close to his home,
was in a similar condition to this run-down and
derelict one.

Organising concerts was something John had
done many times before for a number of good
causes, working alongside his old school friend
Kenny Herbert, who was not only a talented
musician, but had an uncanny resemblance to
Paul McCartney in looks and sound. Kenny and
his new wife Caroline had been offered a free
place to stay on the island by John, for their
honeymoon, if he would be up for performing a
Beatles tribute evening for one night. John would
set up the venue, lights, and sound system. Kenny

would provide backing tracks and perform a set of Beatles hits. The deal was done. Tickets were advertised in Focus and on posters, food and drink vendors paid to be there on the night and the money was now flowing in.

The concert was a great success and it attracted old and young who all loved the music and Kenny's performance. The fundraising target of 10,000 euros was nearing its total and soon there would be enough in the bank to purchase everything that was needed. The dream of every boy on the island was to have a decent football pitch, but on the arid island, the only grass which would grow required a permanent sprinkler system and water was a scarce commodity, especially in summer, when it was needed most. The girls wanted a football pitch too, as they had started their own team, but they also had other wishes, swings, a flying fox, a concert area or theatre and clean toilets with doors on the cubicles which would keep the boys out. The girls had much more imagination than the boys. The planning group had tried to include as much on the wish list as was humanly possible.

The first thing to do, before any work started, was to make sure no dangerous items were on the ground and to everyone's surprise, eight syringes were found and placed in safe containers. The broken seats were removed and those who used to hang around in the park in the evening soon moved on to another more discreet location. A JCB digger owned by the cousin of the *Sugar* restaurant owner was used to clear and smooth down the entire area, before lorryloads of coarse sand and fine gravel were delivered, and under John's strict supervision the landscape started to evolve. He was presented with a yellow hard hat and was christened Bob the Builder by the locals.

He enjoyed his new role, and it brought back happy memories of working with his father in the family building business which at its peak employed over 25 men in all trades. Supervising builders and using surveying, and accurate measuring equipment, was in his blood and a crude water level made from a clear plastic hose allowed him to set out the area as he wanted. Unlike many bosses, he always treated his men as equals, which made him a popular employer, but it made it more difficult for him when, during quiet spells in the industry, he had to make some of his men redundant. It was hard to make anyone redundant at the best of times, when they would easily find work elsewhere, but much harder when the entire industry was quiet, and John knew that the employee was a husband, father, and the breadwinner in the family. It was never an easy job, and it was now something he did not miss.

Because of the lack of timber on the island, most of the playground equipment was produced by a local blacksmith and he was more than happy with the order for over 2,000 euros' worth of work. The lorryloads of gravel and sand and use of the JCB would amount to another 1,000 Euros and the balance of the funds raised would be spent on the contractor who was to provide basic toilets and shower facilities. Fortunately, a water supply existed, and a reliable second-hand solar water panel provided hot, or at least warm, water. The question of the sprinkler system and grass was left unanswered.

As the project was nearing completion, John was keen to make sure all the contractors received prompt payment. Another thing he had learned from running his own business. The job was not over until everyone was paid. He went to the bank in Pothia to withdraw the money to pay the contractors, from the account he had set up to keep the fundraising separate from his own finances and he could not believe his ears when the teller said there was nothing in the account.

Assuming that it had been a clerical error, as even banks in the UK had been less than efficient in his experience, especially the Clydesdale Bank who he won a case against for financial incompetence. He was nevertheless still concerned. The branch manager, Ron, which was the first syllable of an unpronounceable much longer Greek name, was summoned, and as John could by now easily translate their conversation. He understood everything, long before the manager explained it to him in broken English. The account had not been cleared out and transferred into another account. All payments John had a record of paying into the account had in fact gone into another account. John had nothing he could withdraw.

After the discussion with Ron and the arguments had subsided, he left the bank, feeling dazed and confused. Everyone in the bank had heard the heated discussions. By the end of the day the talk in every café and shop in Pothia, and probably the rest of the island, was about the missing money.

News travelled fast on the small island, and nothing travelled faster than a scandal involving money – possibly with the exception of those involving sex.

It did not take long for the rumours to take a nasty turn, inspired by Nick the Mayor, to add fuel to the fire by suggesting, always indirectly, that John had cleared out the account and that that had been his plan all along. He probably always had the intention of fleecing the islanders, *the tourist* was just like all the others, looking for a way to help himself at the expense of the locals, which was the general thrust of every contribution Nasty Nick made to the debate.

John immediately offered to repay the amount to the account from his own finances until the issue could be cleared up. He thought that 10,000 euros would not break the bank and he would still have to work hard to find out where the money had gone. This was his first mistake.

Many, including some of his new friends on the island, assumed that the offer to repay the missing money was an admission of guilt. After all, if he had not taken it in the first place, why would anyone offer to repay the money they had not taken?

The history of crime on the island was that the suspect only ever offered to repay money stolen, after they had been clearly found guilty of the crime, in the hope that it might reduce their sentence. Anyone suspected of theft, or any other crime on Kalymnos and claiming their innocence, never offered to do anything other than proclaim they had been the victim of the crime, by being accused in the first instance.

Even well-known crooks caught red-handed would wail about how their reputation had been damaged by the accusation, despite the CCTV evidence showing them caught in the act.

The contractors were all paid, the playground equipment installed and the *piece de resistance* was about to be unfurled, or unrolled, in the park, but the shine on the entire project had been left seriously tarnished. Hardly a day passed without some comment or innuendo being made at his expense, and the pleasure of being on the island turned slowly to pain.

He felt that if he had been charged with stealing the cash, he would at least have a chance of proving his innocence. This was much worse. Without being charged with any crime, he had been found guilty in the court of public opinion on the island. There was no appeal and not even a chance of parole. He felt like exile was the sentence. He would have to leave the island. "What was the point in staying?" he thought.

John had arranged a small team of men and trucks, paid for out of his own pocket, to finish the job, as he could not raise the issue of finance with anyone now.

That evening, the container on the harbour side was unlocked and some small equipment was put into the van John had hired for the day. Behind the smaller equipment, the long rolls of artificial turf looked like giant green Swiss-rolls with black cream between each layer. Each roll was carefully dragged out of the container and craned onto the two trucks as the sun began to set. Few people were around as he could not face the prospect of any problems at this stage of the game. All it needed was Nasty Nick to appear with some official form about customs clearance or local import tax and he would be locked up for tax evasion - if his recent luck was anything to go by.

The last truck was loaded, and the crane followed them to the now nearly-finished playpark with all the new equipment installed and toilets and showers working well.

The rolls of artificial grass were craned off the trucks and lowered into position in the park. John had taken detailed instructions about how to ensure a good finish, how to trim and fix the artificial turf in position and how to make sure it stayed that way. The men hired were on a fixed sum and would only be paid when the job was finished and perfect. They worked long into the night, supervised by John, and when the last of the sunset had finally gone, the lights from their cars and vans were supplemented by the bank of lights on the roof of the crane. The job was finished at 5 am and the men were paid in full. As the sun rose John could admire the perfect finish on the football pitch, the play area, and the mini amphitheatre for concerts.

Tom and Suzie from Telendos never at any time doubted John's integrity and honesty and while the playpark group had stopped meeting since the financial scandal, Tom and Suzie were always there to support John, who was now, more often than not, on his own. They were made custodians of the bags of fine rubber granules needed to top up the grass to keep it in good condition. They were also given the white line machine and the keys to the lock-up storing the surplus 'grass' to be used for repairs and they were left with the tools to do those repairs. John was not going to let this park deteriorate, as many others on the island had done. This one reminded him of the grass at Kew Gardens in London – perfect.

As the sun rose, he looked at his watch and he had just enough time to go over to *Sugar* for his favourite breakfast, a Kalymnion salad, fresh fruit, Greek yoghurt, sprinkled with muesli and topped with locally made honey, washed down with fresh orange juice and finished with coffee. He watched and studied the faces of everyone as they passed. Some drivers swerved as they took in the view.

The complete amazement on the faces of the children on their way to school, who ran over, touched, stroked, and felt the grass they thought had grown overnight. Others rolled about on it, and the park soon filled up with children and adults who should have been well on their way, but today would be late and would have a story to tell. The owner of *Sugar* had seen it all unfold throughout the night and he hugged John and would not hear of him paying for his meal. It felt to him like his last supper.

He drove back to the house to drop off the few packages and to pick up his bag, before locking up, hiding the keys in the wishing well outside and heading to the harbour to drop off the hired van, just in time to catch the early morning ferry to Mastahari.

Down at the harbour one friend had not deserted him. Bobby was looking up with a quizzical look on his grubby face, as if to say, "What's going on?" He gave Bobby a hug as he looked back on the town He felt a knot in his stomach, it could be worse he thought, not sure exactly how much worse it could actually be. He was going home. Carol would be busy painting and he would see Sarah and the girls again. It was maybe not so bad after all.

Looking down through his binoculars, one man was already celebrating. Nasty Nick had won. *The tourist* was beaten. He could now plan his re-election. In his mind, he was saying, "four more years... four more years."

John arrived in Mastahari on the early morning regular ferry. The bustling harbour area now had the regular and sunset cruise ferry owner being kept busy with a full load of passengers. He was now offering premium morning 'dolphin watching cruises' to Kalymnos with breakfast included, as an alternative to the basic ferry used by the locals and the many Kalymnions who now worked on Kos.

He doffed his black captain's cap to John, knowing that John had changed his fortune.

The driver taking the near-full bus load of tourists to the ferry smiled and offered John a free lift to Kos airport. "Thanks for the opportunity, this bus service has changed my life." The harbourmaster ducked out of the way as John walked by.

At the airport, the team was as efficient as ever, though the leaflets needed a few improvements, he thought.

Wiry rock climbers were now coming in significant numbers since Bruce added a new site specifically aimed at the off-season climbing community. John's idea of getting the climbers to submit photos to the Focus resulted in some spectacular climbing photos ending up on the climbers' website. A map containing climbs and the mystery of their grades was also on the site. Kalymnos had become something of a Mecca in the climbing world and one enterprising climber planned to open a climbing supplies shop. And for the children, at least they had one decent park to play in.

Maybe if Maria and Hope go back next year, they will enjoy it too. He smiled as he thought of their faces, which he was now looking forward to seeing in four or five hours.

Chapter 10
Back Home

Arriving back at Edinburgh, John was braced for the icy blast, which was part of the welcome to Scotland for many visitors. There is no such thing as bad weather, only the wrong clobber, his friend Claire would say. She enjoyed hiking in Wales and knew all about bad weather. John was wearing the right clobber for a sunny day in Greece and had convinced himself that one day it would be lovely and warm when he walked out of Edinburgh airport, and that this would be that day. He was wrong.

Within 20 minutes his taxi pulled up outside his home in the western suburbs of Edinburgh. He always stopped for a moment to take in the setting of their home.

Tucked away behind a 400-year-old beehive-shaped dovecot, with space for over 1000 nests, was the former home of Scotland's only tapestry weaving workshop and design studio, built by the Marquis of Bute in 1912 to house the weavers of the Dovecot Studio. Not long after the opening, the studio was rocked by World War I in 1914, when two of the master weavers headed to the front, never to return. None of the apprentices had a chance to complete their seven-year apprenticeships and when the Dovecot Studio closed in 1916, they would have to wait until the studio reopened in 1919 to return to work.

After many years, the tapestry weaving studio moved to a city centre location and the building was then converted into two open-plan houses in 2003. The West Wing, as it was known until the Post Office gave it an official number, was just what Carol and John had dreamed of. A mix of a country cottage and a loft apartment and in the perfect location. They put in an offer before the conversion was completed and, in the summer of 2003, moved into their new home.

John and Carol always felt they had more space than they really needed and when Maria was born two years later in Greece and then needed specialist medical care in Edinburgh, Sarah and her new family decided to return to Scotland permanently. They were welcomed into the new house, while they saved up a deposit for a place of their own.

Carol was now back home from Africa, working in her studio and building up a collection of paintings for her next solo exhibition at the Scottish Ornithologists' Centre, near Aberlady, outside

Edinburgh. It had hosted Carol's three best-selling solo exhibitions and the curator, Dave Allen, was keen to have one final solo exhibition by Carol before his impending retirement. Like Dave, Carol was planning to scale down her workload in the near future, and the move from full-time to part-time work meant this exhibition would probably be her last for a while.

She had known from phone calls about the missing money for the park, but only realised when John walked in the door how much it had taken out of him. He had lost weight, aged badly, and looked as if he had been completely drained of all energy.

It did not take John long to regain his mojo and get back into enjoying life in Edinburgh. The Edinburgh Festival was about to start, and the city was at its best, with several thousand shows being staged during the month of August.

A surprise phone call from an old friend, Nick Hayes, would give John his first-ever opportunity to perform in the Festival, which was the world's largest arts festival.

Nick was the musical director of a male voice choir who had been rehearsing a show called *Twa Rebellions* and because of throat problems, the narrator had to pull out, leaving the entire show at risk. Nick was looking for someone with a strong Scottish voice, who could narrate the story of Bonnie Prince Charlie and the 1745 rebellion. There was nothing difficult to learn, as the narrator could hold a book and read the story. Stage direction and timing would have to be rehearsed. John was up for it and before the end of the month would be performing on a new stage.

The Festival and the *Twa Rebellions* gave John just the refreshing break he needed and in September his thoughts were returning to Kalymnos, when the phone rang. It was Tom and Suzie from Telendos, who explained that the island had been gripped by a court case and the discovery that a bank employee had revealed that he had been forced to move money from different accounts by the Mayor of Kalymnos. A bank audit had revealed what had been going on.

There had not been enough hard evidence to charge the Mayor, but the bank employee, Ron, had gone into great detail as to how he had moved money into different accounts on behalf of the Mayor, who was also the treasurer of the island council. At times, the Mayor would move council balances into high-interest accounts and then months later return the original sums to the council, leaving the interest in his personal accounts. At other times he would use council deposits to purchase properties from those who had fallen on hard times, to buy their homes at

knock-down prices. Sometimes they would be re-
sold later the same day for ten or twenty thousand
euros more, as they were sold to purchasers at
nearer the market price, leaving the profit in one
of the Mayor's many accounts.

Some of those who had sold their homes at
below market value were suffering from serious
illness, others had been unemployed. Buying a
house at below market value was not a crime, but
it was not what anyone expected their elected
representatives to be doing – and with their
money.

One of the transactions was to move money into
the Kalymnos 'parks and recreation' fund from
another park fund. The Mayor had assured the
bank employee that this was all perfectly legal,
but the fund account emptied was for the park
being renovated by John and his team and the
funds were clearly not stolen by John, as some
had thought, but used by the Mayor for his pet
projects, including the council-owned park near his
own home.

The Mayor was not charged or convicted, but
the islanders realised that what he had done was
morally reprehensible. He was a guilty man and
the islanders realised that a great injustice had
been done to John.

They wanted to apologise to him in person. Tom was asked to relay this message to Edinburgh and to ask John if he would return to Kalymnos for one more visit.

Back in his home office, autumn had arrived and the leaves on his Acer trees had turned bright red, and golden brown on the many others he could look out upon. He was now back into a routine, writing most mornings and making steady progress on his life's story. Spending so much time on the computer had given him a stiff back and the doctor prescribed more exercise. Carol had wanted to get a dog for many years and John was mellowing to the idea. The fate of Bobby on Kalymnos began to prey on his mind.

A quick visit to Kalymnos to say hello to old friends and end the bad feeling that had been around when he last left and to see Bobby once more would make a trip worthwhile.

He hated the thought of bad blood remaining and wanted to clear the air, once and for all, but did not really want to return to the island for long. The love he once had for it had gone.

He went on to Bruce's website and within minutes

had booked his flight, hired a car, and confirmed his ferry link to Kalymnos. He read a few reviews and noticed that some of the accommodation was fully booked. "Something must be working well," he thought, with a wry smile on his face.

Chapter 11
Bobby

The flight was on time, the airport in Kos was mobbed and chaotic, the team was still there making new visitors aware of the delights of Kalymnos. John was welcomed by one of the original team members and within half an hour, was on the ferry. No dolphins this time and for the first time, a dark cloud was hanging over the island.

The most welcome sight he could hope for was there, when he saw Bobby on the quay. "People here have let me down, but you never have, Bobby," he spoke quietly and was convinced his best friend understood every word he had said.

His first stop was to the island pet shop to buy a new collar for Bobby and to make it clear who his owner was. Some of the best dog food available and a stainless-steel bowl finalised the deal. They were now partners for life. Bobby stuck with John from then on.

His next meeting was with Tom and Suzie at the Olympic Hotel, on the opposite side of the harbour from the Mayor's office. John sat at an outside table, ordered a beer, and stared over to Nick's office. He could not see the figure in the shadows but was convinced he was there. Bobby sat in the shade of his table and would be ready to defend his new master from any threat, if needed. In the meantime, he would enjoy his prime meaty chunks and a cool drink of water from his shiny new bowl

Tom explained how the island had come to life and how John's ideas had turned the island economy, and the islanders' spirits, around. The tourists were returning in greater numbers, the website was responsible for increased trade each month, the team on Kos was as effective as ever, the rock climbers were there in the off-season, the ferry was often full, the hotels and restaurants had never had it so good, and the children were loving and caring for their new park. Work on the new pedestrian lanes had started, and work renovating the derelict buildings was now steadily moving forward, and was showing results. Some of the small shops had already been let for the following summer and people were feeling optimistic for the first time in years. Despite all this, life for many and the potential on the island were being strangled by the Mayor and his cronies on the Island Council.

The *Focus* newsletter had become dormant - it was still being produced but had lost any direction. It was now mostly full of adverts and many volunteer distributors had given up, as their loyalty to it was not based on delivering an advertising sheet. For a long time, people had felt let down by their elected representatives. Promises made had been broken time and time again. Nobody wanted to speak out for fear of reprisals. Jobs in key areas were still tightly controlled by the Mayor and a thriving island was not what he wanted, if it loosened his grip on it. He did not want change, he wanted things to stay the same and that included his remaining in office.

Tom put it to John that as the elections for Mayor were due the following May if a new candidate with all the right credentials could be found and elected, the island would, at last, have a chance of moving into the 21st Century. He had his finger on the pulse of the islanders and they were not willing to settle for things remaining as they were any longer.

There was a particular groundswell of support for change on the island from women, who were no longer prepared to be second-class citizens and wanted change now, so that their daughters had the same opportunities as their sons would have. "What they were asking for was what was fair, and they will accept nothing less," Tom added.

That phrase made the hairs on the back of John's neck rise up.

He had first heard it in a speech by Russell Johnston, the veteran Scottish Liberal MP, many years ago and it had struck John over the decades as the test he could apply to any injustice. It was at the heart of why he was involved in politics.

All he would demand in any situation, for anyone, or group of people, was what was fair – but he would accept nothing less. He included the phrase in a few speeches he had made at Westminster and hearing Tom say it, reminded him that fighting injustice was one fight he would never run away from.

Looking down at Bobby, they both knew they would soon have a battle on their hands. "This is war," he whispered. Bobby tilted his head and barked, as if to say, "Count me in."

A phone call was then made back to Carol, saying that, like Captain Oates, he might be gone for quite some time.

Bobby.

Chapter 12
Planning the Campaign

As an election agent and campaign organiser John, and other agents, had often used the phrase, "the candidate was just a legal necessity, it was the agents who really won elections". As the years passed, John realised that a good agent and campaign organiser was important, as it had been a key factor in his electoral success, but that the right candidate was also essential, and had to inspire the team and deliver the campaign that he and the agent, would devise.

If the Mayor of Kalymnos was to be replaced at the next election, John knew that he was able to develop a good campaign, but without the right candidate they would struggle, as the incumbent was often more difficult to remove than many people expected. It was impossible to quantify the personal vote anyone in office had built up, as it could come from a mixture of loyalty, friendship, respect, and thanks for helping with an issue, and over the years this could make enough difference in a tight race to stop the challenger winning.

Rather than planning to get someone elected, John was keen to build a movement of people who wanted something better and who shared the same ideals. If they believed in something, they would work for it, and hopefully the right candidate would emerge in time. Many people who wanted to get elected were exactly the wrong people to stand for election, as their interest was often more about promoting themselves than campaigning on behalf of others.

John had become dismayed by modern campaigning techniques and the dumbing down of elections in order to appeal to the lowest common denominator. Lots of photos of a smiling individual candidate in glossy literature would not be at the heart of this campaign. He had never lost an election campaign in his life, and he was not about to start now.

He felt a spring in his step as his thoughts returned to the campaign trail. Six months was not long, but it was enough time to get it right.

It was now October; the elections were in May and there would be a break from campaigning over Christmas as it was never a wise move to disturb family or religious celebrations at that time of year. People out campaigning at Christmas also risked being seen as slightly strange and without a real life.

Before the final month-long campaign there was a lot to do. Nominations would open in early April and until then many people would say they were standing for election but would never actually do so. In order to be on the ballot paper, certain criteria had to be satisfied. The nominee had to be on the electoral register, had to either live or work on the island, must not be an Island Council employee, must not have outstanding debts to the Council, and must have the signature of support from ten registered electors in order for the nomination to be valid. After nominations had closed, papers checked and the final list of candidates who would be on the ballot paper confirmed, he wanted to make sure everything that could be done had been done. Game on.

Before starting any campaign planning, John spent some time travelling around the island, meeting people, chatting in cafes, visiting and catching up with old friends and seeing just exactly what was unfolding on the island. His hired car was an open-topped Suzuki and Bobby was by his side every step of the way, with his new collar on and the wind whistling through his hair, as they negotiated the cliff-top roads around the island. A couple of weeks of getting up to speed with everyone and every issue left John well-prepared and ready for action.

Good elections can be won and lost by individuals,

but the best election results and the most enjoyable elections are won by getting a good team in place. Knowing that others are working towards the same goal and fitting the pieces of the jigsaw together was one of the most satisfying feelings he had experienced, and when it resulted in the right man or woman being elected, it would be the start of what was needed to deliver the change the island craved.

Being elected was not the end, as many people thought, it was just the start of delivering on the promises made during the election and then working to improve the lives of those you were elected to represent.

It was impossible to keep everyone happy, but doing your best, was all that anyone could ask for. Listening was at the heart of the process and making tough decisions would make it something that not everyone was up to, but good leadership was something most people appreciated and finding that candidate would be a top priority.

A small team met at campaign HQ, as Sarah's house had become known. Although John wanted everyone to play their part, each member of the group knew that John was the one who would make the key decisions.

Getting the *Focus on Kalymnos* back up and

running, with good local stories full of interesting news and information was the first priority. John's name would be included as the new editor, and he would write a short piece about his return to the island. Photographs of the park development and children enjoying the new facilities along with the story of how it had all happened would be the number one story. A small mention would be made about the money, but nothing in detail. John knew that what he wanted to show was what could be achieved by people working together for the common good. Most people were aware of the Mayor's involvement and his part in the financial scandal surrounding the park and they assumed he was involved in other dodgy accounting practices, but this was not the time to raise the issue.

The old team of distributors would need to be contacted. The target would be to get many more people on the island involved, but in the meantime having 10 people who would each be responsible for one-tenth of the delivery would be enough.

Small teams would go out into each area with 1,000 *Focus* newsletters and the feeling of camaraderie would develop as each team was built up. No house was to be missed and the production would continue in English and Greek, as before. A novel twist was to have the front and back pages printed back to front and upside down so that whatever language version was being read, it felt as if it was on the front page.

Production of the first edition was easy, as there was much going on and the task was to edit the stories and photos to make it interesting enough to engage with the islanders and get them talking about the issues raised. It took little time to produce and as the team went out on the streets the response was immediate. More distributors were soon volunteering and the target of fifty helpers looked like it would be achievable before too long.

"Houses don't vote." John captured the attention of the team with a statement of the obvious. While the distributors had been out delivering to every part of the island he had been exploring the electoral register at the local registry office.

This was something few people showed interest in, and the Registrar for the island was more than happy to explain the details of electoral registration on Kalymnos, which understandably was not the hot topic for discussion in local tavernas. "Twenty per cent of the islanders are not on the electoral register, and you can guarantee every supporter of the Mayor is. This is something we need to deal with before the December deadline." Only those on the electoral register by 31st December would be allowed to vote in the local elections in May.

Back in the United Kingdom, when elections were held in May, the electoral register was open for new additions until the middle of April. Making sure every supporter was on the register was a key part of the campaign. Not only was it important to make sure every supporter was on the register, but it was also vitally important that they voted on the day. If they were away or unable to vote on election day, postal or proxy votes would be arranged for them.

Allowing later additions to the register ensured that as the interest in the campaign increased and the media and campaign coverage began to engage the voters, if they were not on the register, they could make sure their names were added. The Registrar explained that the December deadline was there for historical reasons and had never been changed to take into account how times had changed. In days gone by, many fishermen would be away for long spells at sea but would always be back at home to celebrate Christmas and the New Year with their families. Part of the tradition on the island was to make sure that during that time at home a few family matters were also dealt with, such as renewing house insurance policies and making sure those men were on the register as they would not only vote, but they would also let their family know how they should vote too. Times had changed but the deadline remained the same.

John knew that this could be the Achilles heel of the campaign, as he was sure that, as in most places, few people would be interested in local elections in the run-up to Christmas and by the time the campaigns were underway and they were talking about who to vote for, if they realised they were not registered and so could not vote, it would be too late to add their names to the register.

If a story about this appeared in the next *Focus*, or the team went out and about trying to get new names added on to the register, it would be too obvious that something was going on and the plan was to keep this under wraps until it was a fait accompli.

One of John's new recruits was a mild-mannered man called Stavros, who was the head-teacher at the island's secondary school. He had seen at first hand the devastation his beloved education system had suffered at the hands of an incompetent Education Committee of the Island Council which was more interested in photo opportunities in the local press of the school prize-giving, with the Committee members grinning like Cheshire cats, than the real value of education being the prize for every child.

He was particularly incensed at the lack of special needs provision for those children who were not able to cope with every day or standard tasks. For too long, children who were anything other than perfect were hidden away or sent to an orphanage and he was on the point of retiring and leaving education altogether, when the thought of one last chance to change things came his way.

Strictly speaking, he should have remained neutral and should not have been involved with anything affecting his job or the education of the children, but he took the view that remaining neutral was in fact supporting the status quo, so he had no choice but to get involved with John and the team. He knew from the start that this was a political revolution on the island and that all revolutions needed undercover agents. He would be their spy.

After much discussion about how to extend the franchise throughout the island, while not exposing that it was the campaign group that was behind it, Stavros came up with the answer. "Democracy. Demos – the people, and Kratos – power. The power of the people. This is on the school curriculum, and I will want every family of every child in my school to participate in this greatest of gifts, given to the world by the Greeks, before the end-of-year deadline. Leave it to me." He smiled. The rest of the group was stunned into silence. The quiet man was turning up the volume. Their first problem had a possible solution and a man with a mission, who was now on the case. Time to crack open a bottle of Chablis, kept for every successful occasion – and this was the first. As they enjoyed a cool glass of John's favourite wine, a mischievous Stavros added, "I might even ask the Mayor to come to the school to talk about the importance of democracy." The team erupted in laughter at the very thought of it.

With the first of the new style *Focus* being delivered, the feedback forms started to come back in. The distributors were starting to organise into small subgroups with each having one spokesman to feedback to a meeting of all the spokesmen to find out if the same issues were cropping up in different parts of the island. The remote areas had completely different concerns from the towns, but everyone was fed up with the potholes in the roads, causing accidents and repairs to springs and shock absorbers on many cars and vans. The only people happy with the state of the roads were the garage owners, but even they now realised that they would rather their customers could spend their money on what they wanted at their garages, not on the same repairs time and time again.

John had decided that every person who filled in a feedback form would get a personal reply signed by him. Some would be in English and others in Greek, but everyone would know their view had been listened to.

John's spoken Greek was now much improved, but his written Greek was not as good as he would have liked, so he decided that he would have to set up a system similar to what he had when he was a Member of Parliament, in order to deal with the growing volume of casework he was attracting.

Some MPs saw casework, or dealing with issues on behalf of individuals, as a pain in the neck, or a chore that distracted them from their "real" work at Westminster. John always viewed this work as being at the heart of the reason he was elected: to work on behalf of his constituents, whoever they voted for or supported.

After stepping down from Parliament, he lost count of the number of people who approached him and said thanks for dealing with, or doing his best to deal with their problems, on all issues, whether large or small. The number of constituents who left the letter from their MP, with the House of Commons Portcullis logo, on their mantle-piece as a proud reminder that they had had a personal letter from their MP, was one of the many reasons that John's majority rocketed when he stood for re-election.

While the rest of the team and many of the locals saw the feedback form as simply that, John knew it was much more. It gave him a reason to write to individuals on a topic of their choosing, of their concern. It provided their name and address, and increasingly it provided their email address, as the use of email had grown especially in the more outlying areas. Most importantly of all, it provided the start of a discussion on the doorstep. The email list had grown and many of those on the email list had opted in to receive updates on a range of issues from John. This was another growing list of people who fed in a range of concerns and issues they would like to see improved on the island.

It would be impossible to keep on top of every issue and every piece of correspondence without a good system and he knew just the man to set it up.

Ewan Irvine worked for John from not long after his election to Parliament. Unlike most senior jobs, where employees are supplied with an office, support staff, computer, office furniture and all the normal requirement to do the job, MPs were supplied with a budget and had to arrange everything themselves.

This is one of the reasons for the expenses scandal which rocked the British Parliament and led to the imprisonment of a number of Labour MPs. Even when he was elected to the Edinburgh City Council, there was a desk, a secretary, a phone, and a computer waiting to be used by him.

The Westminster system meant that at Westminster new MPs were walking around the corridors of the Houses of Parliament holding bundles of mail, while looking for a spare table in the canteen to open it. John had offered his election agent, Stephen, a job at Westminster if elected, and from day one he had a sharp young man working with him to set up a new office in London.

In Edinburgh, after John's election, there was not only any office furniture, but there was also no office. For many new MPs this proved to be a major problem as there was little support and most had no idea how to deal with this problem. Having leased property before, John had seen this coming.

During the election campaign he had found a suitable empty property to be used for his campaign headquarters in the heart of the constituency and he also negotiated a good rent with the landlord in the event of him becoming the new MP, in return for free use of the premises for the final two months of his campaign. On the day of his election, his campaign office turned into the MP's office and as soon as the celebration party was over, the office was up and running while he headed for London to take the oath to the Queen and officially become a Member of Parliament.

He knew Ewan as an active community worker,

who worked for Standard Life Insurance, but really wanted a job where he could help people. John offered Ewan the role of caseworker, by allaying Ewan's worries and saying they would both have to learn on the job. Ewan worked with John throughout his entire time at Westminster and in recent years had given up work to care for his ailing mother, and to develop his other interests.

Although Ewan looked like he could handle himself, he had a very gentle nature, so John decided not to mention that there were risks working for an MP, especially dealing with awkward constituents and that some MPs' constituency staff had in the past been attacked by those constituents who had snapped, or who had a range of other problems in their life that could not be solved by a visit to see their MP.

John phoned Ewan to offer him a few weeks in Greece, lots of wine or beer and good fun, if Ewan would set up his casework system. John also asked him to bring the campaigning software programme and a new laptop which would allow him to build up a database of every elector on the island. Canvassing had already begun, and the information collected would be a key part of the campaign.

Canvassing, or door-knocking is what politicians say they do, but very few actually do it. Often, they will use the phrase, "When I am knocking on doors," or "My constituents often tell me," when they want to statement and to give it some more authenticity than by just saying, "I think." That would not sound as impressive and does not say, "man of the people."

John actually enjoyed getting out and about, delivering *Focus* newsletters or doing street surveys in order to get the views of people throughout his constituency. With over 100,000 people in Edinburgh West, he had to work hard, supported by a dedicated band of helpers, to make an impact and he felt that it took nearly seven years to finally be widely recognised. His constant disdain was for young campaigners who would fight one election, over a few months, or a year, and think they were known by everybody and set to win, only to come third or fourth on election night.

Street surveys consisted of delivering a leaflet to every house early in the week, saying the team, including John, would be back later in the week at a specific time and if the householder wanted to discuss anything, they should put the back of the first leaflet in their window, which consisted of John's name and a big tick. This would also weed out those who were in the opposite camp, as they would not want to look as if they had put up a poster supporting their opposition. Usually, a handful of people would be contacted personally, but everyone in the street was leafleted twice in one week, as everyone got a second leaflet on the second visit.

Everyone was also made aware that they had someone who was taking the time to visit them, and they knew they were being contacted by the person elected to represent them. For most people, this was the first time in their lives that they had ever met an elected politician. It was now time to start street and village surveys on Kalymnos.

As the weeks passed, it was becoming increasingly obvious that John was doing everything a candidate should do, but he still had no intention of standing for election and remaining on the island for the future. His plan was to find a candidate who was eligible for election, and this meant working or living on the island.

The team was content to let John run things and the growing band of helpers looked to John for ideas and leadership but having been elected in a city with half a million people and then to Parliament at Westminster he really did not want to return to local politics full time, even if he was eligible to stand.

Then he had a brainwave. Why not let the Mayor

think he was planning to stand as the candidate against him, as no doubt even Nasty Nick, or one of his advisors, would then know he could spike their campaign at the last minute by declaring that John was neither on the electoral roll as a resident nor did he have a job on the island. One of these was essential for him to stand for election as Mayor of Kalymnos.

The issue of who would be the candidate would have to be put on the back burner, as Ewan was due to arrive the next morning and one spare bedroom needed to be organised for him. The next morning as John and Bobby waited for Ewan's arrival at the ferry, his phone rang, and Ewan announced he would not be on the ferry as expected. He would be arriving in a yacht crewed by a group of muscular good-looking men.

Ewan had discovered a charter sailing company for gay men, with a gay crew who would look after his every need. By the time the yacht arrived at the marina, Ewan had a new "friend," Vangelis, who offered to stay and help Ewan deal with any translation difficulties for a couple of weeks. Ewan had fortunately remembered the computer and software.

By breakfast time the next day, Ewan was single again. Nobody asked what had happened to Vangelis, but this meant that there would be fewer distractions in the weeks ahead, or so he thought.

Normally fundraising was an important issue in every campaign, but hard as John tried to think of ways the campaign would spend money, people would think of ways to save money or to raise money.

The advertising in *Focus* was more than paying for its production cost. The printing of more political literature had been taken care of by the offer of a colour photocopier and the ink was on order. The design of eye-catching posters and a campaign website were being worked on by Bruce back in Edinburgh, as thanks for his now money-making holiday booking site. His income was growing steadily and following on from the success of his new website, other enquiries had given him his busiest year yet. He had also found software which produced everything simultaneously in English and Greek, without understanding a word of it.

Chapter 13
Democracy

Stavros's idea of inviting the Mayor to school to speak to the school assembly about Democracy clearly inspired the Mayor to take this further and instead, he instructed the Island Council to organise a public meeting in the town hall, which was able to hold the largest possible meeting on the island, at which there would be a number of speakers, all of whom would say what a great person the Mayor was. The highlight of the evening would be a speech from Nick himself, The Mayor of Kalymnos. Council employees and their families were warned that this was one event they should not miss and rousing support in the style of North Korea would be expected.

Posters went up around the island and it looked like the starting pistol for the election had been fired. It was not yet Christmas but things were not looking too good for John and his team. They were making regular contact with people around the island, they knew the issues they were concerned with, a strong team was being built, and more new distributors were more than enough to replace the old ones who had given up.

Ewan's decision to stay longer on the island resulted in an effective computer system of logging all cases against the entire electoral roll. Stavros's democracy campaign had resulted in an awareness of the importance of being on the roll before the year's end in order to be able to vote in May. Support was growing. Fundraising was not an issue. Something was missing, there was no "buzz", and an event was needed to excite people and to make them want to vote, as a low turnout of voters on the day could be a disaster. He knew that elections can be lost because of apathy and there was a danger that, like many local elections, apathy might win on the day.

The Mayor, on the other hand, had posters all around the island with his face on them, advertising his big pre-Christmas public meeting on Democracy. No candidate had been declared by the 'troublemakers' on the island. He had been the Mayor while the island had enjoyed its economic revival and he felt like the man of the moment – a man who was heading for re-election in May. He was confident – too confident.

As Christmas approached the Island Council hosted its annual Christmas Party, with invitations to those and such as those, businessmen, community leaders, Councillors and other wealthy or influential people on the island, all hosted by the Mayor, who would personally welcome the guests and then make yet another speech, after a sumptuous meal and before the music and dancing began. Everyone would be in good spirits and there would be plenty of spirit flowing on the evening.

John was amazed to receive an invitation to the event. "Know your enemy," he thought and he immediately accepted and phoned Carol to let her know to bring a posh frock as well as her Christmas presents. She had insisted that they were going to spend some time together over the Christmas break and he would soon be making a flying visit to Edinburgh, to spend some time with his grandchildren, who, he feared, were starting to forget what he looked like.

John pulled on his dinner jacket and black bow tie, which was rarely used, but was always a winner and as near to a James Bond look as he could get. Carol, never a fan of such events, was prepared to do what was expected and was just glad that this routine was no longer a weekly event. She could cope with it now and again, but she was much more at home out in the African bush.

After the introduction and formalities of the evening were over, John and Carol settled down beside Tom and Susie for the meal, which was produced on a massive barbeque outside. The wine and spirits were flowing, but even at such a supposedly grand event, the bottles were left on the table, something that always irritated John about Greek nights out, and having consumed just too much to drink, he also managed to irritate Nick the Mayor by commenting on his financial transactions in the Parks Department.

The Mayor exploded and lunged at John, who was looking very calm and collected, as he felt even more Bond-like than usual. The Mayor let rip with a rapid-fire of expletives and a Greek monologue that left his guests stunned. He cursed John and foreigners like him, he insulted Carol and all women by revealing his contempt for what he obviously believed were second-class citizens and he said, in Greek, how he had well and truly stitched up John and Ron, the bank employee. In English, he added that he was untouchable, it was his island to do with what he wanted, nobody could challenge him, and nobody ever would.

Seizing his moment, John at first apologised to all the women in the room and stressed that whatever the Mayor had said, his comments were not shared by him, nor would they be by any right-thinking men.

Tom translated this into Greek. John added that this was neither the time nor place to spoil the evening for everyone. Tom translated again and realising that John had understood every word the Mayor had said in Greek, Tom translated the final words of John challenging the Mayor to face him at his public meeting on the value and importance of Democracy.

The Mayor accepted, in front of every important person on the island. There would be no time for any second thought on this.

John had the opportunity he wanted at the upcoming Town Hall meeting to expose the Mayor for what he was and to share it with the rest of the island and to set the campaign on fire.

Chapter 14
The Final Countdown

The music from the old hit by Sparks was playing in his mind. "This Town Ain't Big Enough For Both of Us." Many times, the words of a song would capture exactly what he was feeling and this time he knew that Kalymnos was not big enough for John and Nick. "And it ain't me whose gonna leave." He sang to himself.

Preparation was the key to a successful public meeting. The venue, the people, the acoustics and much more. Everything had to be thought through in detail, with nothing being left to chance.

There was one *Focus* scheduled for delivery before the public meeting and it was packed full of stories which left everyone in no doubt that this would be one night out they would not be going to miss.

Well-organised elections needed to get off the ground before the opposition was ready, and this could be done by preparing the ground and launching a *Flying Start* leaflet. Few others were aware that tonight was the *Flying Start* John had planned.

Many men on the island had planned to attend and were shocked to discover that their wives, daughters, and girlfriends all planned to be there too. Many of the women had kept it to themselves that they were now on the electoral register for the first time, and they were going to make sure their votes counted.

It was obvious that the hall would not hold the expected crowd and speakers were set up along the harbour front to allow those people outside to hear what was going on inside the town hall. John made sure the sound from the speakers could be clearly heard outside the hall and along the entire length of the seafront, so that all those enjoying a meal outside the many harbourside restaurants, bars and tavernas felt like part of the evening. He wanted them all to feel involved.

Many of the locals were used to turning up late for most events and John took advantage of this by making sure his most vocal supporters and those who needed assistance, arrived in plenty of time to get a seat in the main hall. Everyone might hear the debate, but those inside would help set the atmosphere, ask questions, and create the mood for those outside. John wanted to make sure his supporters could do all three. Those outside would hear what was going on inside the hall, and this was no time to allow Nick's rent-a-mob to drown out his voice or his support.

It was a warm evening and John knew that in

the heat of the hall both men would be under pressure, so he wore a light linen shirt and a smart lightweight suit. Sweating never looked good and remembering the reports of the Nixon-Kennedy television debate, he made sure he had an early evening shower and shave before he left. He wanted to look the part, as well as sound right.

An hour before the start time the first of John's supporters started to arrive in the hall and with 30 minutes to go it was filling up nicely.

With 20 minutes to go it was full to capacity with standing room only, and 10 minutes before kick-off the house was jammed.

The sound system was tested, and an announcement was made to let people know that no more space was available in the hall and that those wishing to hear could do so on the PA system, which carried every word clearly along the harbour front.

It was one thing the Mayor had insisted on for his public meetings, to make sure nobody could escape his words, even those who were not at the meeting. To make sure the sound system was working the technician had set it up to play music until the meeting started. It was playing "The Final Countdown" by Europe, an anthem for a fight if ever there was one.

The tension was rising, as was the temperature in the hall. The windows were thrown open and a waft of the cool evening air brought relief to those who had been waiting for the best part of an hour, when the noise in the hall suddenly dropped to a whisper.

The clerk of the council walked onto the stage to make a few housekeeping announcements and was booed off the stage. He pointed to the fire exits but every door was wide open, and every person had heard this speech 10 times before. He then went on to say that the Mayor and John would each have 15 minutes to make their speeches and then there would be one hour of question and answer from the audience and then they each had time to sum up. He would pass around the roving microphone for questions, and he asked everyone to speak clearly.

There were two lecterns on the stage and although they needed no introduction, John and Nick were introduced by the clerk, who was enjoying his moment in the spotlight.

Nick held a sheath of notes and was desperate to get started. He looked hot and sweaty, as usual. He had not bothered to change into fresh clothes and with the hall lights on him, he did not look his best, but it was now too late to do anything about it.

John had made small cards with key facts and figures and a set of bullet points he wanted to get across. He knew the importance of making eye contact with the audience. Reading notes was not a good idea and trying to remember everything risked forgetting some key issues. The cards were small enough to be almost invisible to the audience, but the text was large enough to be read without picking them up. He also had worked long and hard on his final summing up, as he knew that it was vital to leave the audience, inside and outside, with his message ringing in their ears.

The Mayor waxed lyrical about himself, his friends, and his family. He then went on to say what a great job he had done as Mayor and how the island was lucky to have him in the job. He looked at John and referred to the influence tourists had had on the island, how the men could not be trusted and how the women had few moral values. Tourists were sadly a necessary evil, and his job was to exploit them when he could, for the benefit of the island.

Realising that this was supposed to be a discussion about the value of Democracy, he then moved on to why the Greeks had the best systems of government in the world, from Athens to Kalymnos and why, from the Prime Minister to the Mayor, the men Greeks elected were world-class.

He did not realise that every single person he referred to was a man and every time he mentioned anyone in the room, it was a man, and that any opportunities he saw in the future were for their sons. He was slowly but surely ostracising 50% of his audience.

His time was up, but he was confident that John's poor Greek and his use of English, would leave the audience cold. He was feeling confident, as John began to address the crowd.

Starting in English, John welcomed those who had settled on the island but had yet to master the language. He added that for a long time this was exactly how he had felt. He continued with his introduction in English to those islanders and visitors who were outside the hall, who had been totally ignored by the Mayor.

In the bars and restaurants, glasses were being raised by those who were now part of the evening as they could hear every word on the PA system that had been cranked up to make sure they would miss nothing. He complimented the islanders on their unique unspoiled island and their strong family ties.

John continued in English and Greek, to welcome the many women who had joined in, much to the disdain of their menfolk and the younger people who were learning English in school.

At this point he switched to fluent Greek, to welcome the women of the island, who had for so long been told what to do and what to say, by men who should count themselves lucky to be able to share this magnificent island with 50% of the population who have so much more to contribute and who are looking forward to playing their part in the future development of every aspect of Kalymnion life.

To make sure that every daughter has exactly the same opportunity as every son has had for generations. John stopped to take a drink of water and the applause from outside the hall could be heard by all those inside. He had struck a chord and like a gentle wave, it swept towards the hall doors and into the Town Hall where it gathered momentum and it just kept on going. He had connected with his audience. They were listening.

Now it was time to make them think.

The Mayor had been caught off guard, he felt like he had been played for a fool. John had taken a lead, but he had planted questions in the audience to catch John out in the second half of the evening. He was not finished yet.

John had known that Nick's Achilles heel was his

own self-importance, and John made sure that the subject of the evening, Democracy, was properly addressed, but the second point of the evening was to show why Democracy can be abused by those in power to the cost of everyone else.

At no point had Nick taken any time to talk about Democracy. Everything he wanted to say was about himself and in his mind, the point of people voting was to vote for him.

John left his audience with a clear message that the abuse of democratic power was not only wrong, but it must also be fought at every turn by all right-thinking people. For the wrong people to win the day, he reminded them, all it takes is for good men and women to do nothing.

By this time John was aware that the meeting had become a pre-election rally for him and the Mayor, and this is what he had planned all along. The Mayor's disdain for Democracy was clear and his blood pressure was rising. He nodded to the clerk to indicate it was time for questions.

The first question from one of Nick's henchmen was about John's lack of detailed knowledge about the island. What could he say about what mattered here, when his home was thousands of miles away? He was a foreigner, a tourist, no more.

This was an open goal waiting for the ball to be kicked into it. All those feedback forms provided endless examples of what mattered to the people on the island.

John had mastered the way of presenting a list of issues and leaving time for audience response. He left a gap after mentioning the issue, but he also mentioned the name of each person who had raised it. As each person he mentioned had many relatives, and they were all delighted when their family name was mentioned, everyone related in the audience responded to the mention of their family name with a loud cheer. It felt like everyone in the hall had at least one family relative to cheer for.

Realising he was on to a losing run, Nick motioned to another supporter for the second question to be put to John.

"You are a politician from the UK, do you think you could stand for election here?"

Knowing that Nick was aware of his ineligibility to stand in the forthcoming election, John wanted him to think that he would be the candidate, but at no time did John actually confirm his intentions. This left Nick believing that he still held the ace card and that if John submitted his nomination papers they would be rejected at the last minute, leaving Nick to stand unopposed. Re-election would then be a certainty.

John spoke about his track record, his past actions, and why a good leader, a good candidate, can help a community change for the better. He asked people to imagine what the island could be like in the future for them, their children and their grandchildren and he spelt out what made Kalymnos an island worth preserving and the importance of good jobs, which would make the younger people see that they did not have to leave in order to have a future.

He detailed how communication was changing, how jobs were changing, and how with high-speed internet connections, in the future people could work online from anywhere in the world, developing ideas and new businesses. The young people were made aware that since the decline of the sponge fishing industry decades ago, at last they might have a future on their own island.

The many young people who had come along on the evening might still be too young to vote, but they all had an influence on their parents and grandparents, many of whom would. A loud cheer from the youngsters rang out from outside.

Those newly added to the electoral register were also keen to be able to exert their new democratic power and at last, for the first time in their lives, they had heard a vision of the island worth voting for.

When it came to the summing up Nick went first and listed everything he could think of as to why he was a great man and should remain as Mayor, to keep things exactly as they were. At the end, there was a muted rumble from his paid staff and a few others in the hall, and silence from outside.

John followed on. He had taken note of every single issue Nick had used in his summation and detailed exactly why he had failed to deliver what was needed for those on the island. The schools Nick said he was responsible for were poorly maintained with many of the best teachers thinking about retiring or leaving the island, roads which were also the responsibility of the Mayor were full of potholes because of bad quality repairs by his relations company.

Loose gravel on clifftop roads had resulted in serious accidents and deaths. Many parks were a danger to the children who played in them. He listed exactly what the Mayor had admitted responsibility for and then went into great detail as to why he had failed to deliver for the people on every single issue.

He spoke for twice as long as Nick had, to a rapt

audience who wanted more. He knew that the best time to quit is when you are ahead. Leave them wanting more.

He ended by saying. "Nick, you have let down this island, you have let the islanders down. You have lined your own pocket, you have given jobs to family and friends, not to those ablest or most qualified, you have denied able and capable people good jobs and given them to your own friends and family. You have robbed these people of what is rightly theirs, and worst of all, you abused the democratic process. You have used and abused their trust. All the islanders are asking for from their Mayor is what is fair, but they will accept nothing less. It is time for a change. In May the island deserves a new Mayor, and they will get one."

You could have heard a pin drop. Total silence.

Then a wave of applause began, but it was not from in the hall, where people were murmuring to each other. It was a wave of noise from outside, building up slowly from the bars, cafes and tavernas, onto the street, spreading to the crowd outside the hall, until it hit the open doors and windows of the main hall like a tidal surge, and it carried on into the hall from the back, where people suddenly rose to their feet. It was like a Mexican wave, starting at the back row, with the standing ovation eventually hitting the front row.

John stood on the stage looking cool and calm while a hot, furious, and sweating Nick tried and failed to halt the applause. He then slid off the stage and made his exit through a side door.

As he stood on the stage, John raised his hands outstretched to each side as a gesture of thanks. With the glow of the evening sunset from a small window like a spotlight on the back of his head. One old woman fainted, as she was convinced it was a biblical experience. It was the heat.

Watching a united island, ready to back the right candidate to be the next Mayor of Kalymnos. They thought that it would be him, but John knew that he did not need to be the candidate. His work was nearly done.

He had given them hope for a brighter future, hope for a brighter tomorrow. He knew that hope on its own was not enough, but without hope they would give up, he thought to himself. In the words of Harvey Milk, "you have got to give them hope."

He knew that the right person to be elected was not someone who had wanted to be Mayor, or even to get elected, but someone that the islanders wanted to elect as their new Mayor of Kalymnos.

Stavros, Tom, Suzie, and a few others, all had the ability. They could agree amongst themselves who was the best person for the job. Working together they could win the campaign, and change much on the island for the better. End the corruption and nepotism that had become a curse on them all. Give everyone a fair deal.

The team was ready, they had the momentum and John would be their campaign manager, as he had been many times in the past.

He had never lost a campaign before, and he was not about to start now.

THE END

In the May elections, Stavros, the headteacher, who resigned from his job, to allow him to stand for election, is elected as the new Mayor of Kalymnos with an overwhelming majority. With Kalymnos registering the highest voter turnout of any Greek island in a local election.

He immediately announces a plan to ensure all jobs in the Council go to the best applicant and those appointed by the previous Mayor, who were not up to the job they were being paid for, were let go.

He announces several plans for the future, including one to make a provision in all schools on the island for children with disabilities and a rolling programme of playground improvements throughout the island.

John is given the Freedom of Kalymnos award by the Island Council.

The new pedestrian zone goes from strength to strength and new shops, galleries and cafes open up in the former empty buildings.

The Visit Kalymnos website wins best tourist website of the year.

Kenny Herbert starts an annual Beatles Week on the island with Beatles music and tribute bands, and a growing number of fans arriving every year.

John, Carol and Bobby return to Edinburgh, where John finishes writing his story.

Jane's
Studio Press

Made in the USA
Monee, IL
07 November 2022

42f50f33-3a46-4ece-810f-9082f47dd580R01